For David Winford
Invaluable Mentor and Friend

Praise for *Invaluable*

"If you're in business, you need this book! Read it, apply it, and buy *Invaluable* for your entire team. Dave has communicated in a short story what many CEOs wish they could tell their employees, but don't know how. This deeply motivational book is packed with clear action steps to improve one's performance in any organization."
—**Christine Comaford,** CEO, Mighty Ventures

"I encourage you to buy three copies of this wonderful book. Get one for yourself, one for a colleague, and one for a loved one who has lost hope about being 'invaluable'!"
—**Alex Mandossian,** founder,
    ProductiveToday.com

"In this book Dave has brought together a simple yet powerful set of tools that will assist you in cultivating immediate and lasting results! At this point in history it is a key to become invaluable. By using the tools in this book you will truly be able to do so!"
—**Jairek Robbins,** coach, speaker, founder,
    The Jairek Robbins Companies

Invaluable

The Secret to Becoming Irreplaceable

Dave Crenshaw

JOSSEY-BASS
A Wiley Imprint
www.josseybass.com

Published by Jossey-Bass
A Wiley Imprint
989 Market Street, San Francisco, CA 94103-1741—www.josseybass.com

Readers should be aware that Internet Web sites offered as citations and/or
sources for further information may have changed or disappeared between the
time this was written and when it is read.

Limit of Liability/Disclaimer of Warranty: While the publisher and author have
used their best efforts in preparing this book, they make no representations
or warranties with respect to the accuracy or completeness of the contents of
this book and specifically disclaim any implied warranties of merchantability
or fitness for a particular purpose. No warranty may be created or extended
by sales representatives or written sales materials. The advice and strategies
contained herein may not be suitable for your situation. You should consult
with a professional where appropriate. Neither the publisher nor author shall
be liable for any loss of profit or any other commercial damages, including but
not limited to special, incidental, consequential, or other damages.

Jossey-Bass books and products are available through most bookstores. To
contact Jossey-Bass directly call our Customer Care Department within the U.S.
at 800-956-7739, outside the U.S. at 317-572-3986, or fax 317-572-4002.

Jossey-Bass also publishes its books in a variety of electronic formats. Some
content that appears in print may not be available in electronic books.

Library of Congress Cataloging-in-Publication Data

Crenshaw, Dave.
    Invaluable : the secret to becoming irreplaceable / Dave Crenshaw.—1st ed.
        p. cm.
    ISBN 978-0-470-55323-7 (cloth)
    1. Organizational effectiveness. 2. Performance. 3. Value. 4. Time
management. 5. Employee motivation. I. Title.
    HD58.9.C75 2010
    650.1—dc22

                                                            2009051939

Printed in the United States of America
FIRST EDITION

HB Printing   10   9   8   7   6   5   4   3   2   1

CONTENTS

PREFACE

My first book, *The Myth of Multitasking: How "Doing It All" Gets Nothing Done,* grew from need. Early in my career, my clients were all business owners. They came to me feeling starved, desperate for a way to find more time in their days. A quick look at how they were spending their time showed that nearly all were segmenting themselves in too many parts. They had too many job descriptions, too many businesses. Over the course of working with these clients, I developed a program to help them get more time, the most critical aspect of which was to get more focus. Overcoming multitasking is the first great step to overcoming a lack of focus.

From the moment I started my mission to help business owners and CEOs, I found myself working more and more with their employees. Invigorated by their own quick results, business leaders asked me to teach their teams the same principles of success and focus. They wanted their employees to be more productive and, generally speaking, more compliant. In too many cases, the business leader essentially said, "Fix my employees." The underlying message I heard repeatedly from the business leaders was, "If only my employees looked at the business the way I did, everything would be better."

The irony is, as I worked with employees, I would very often hear, "Please fix my boss." Employees would offer example after example of their leader's dysfunctional behavior. "If only he would give clear directions!" "If only she would stop long enough to pay attention to me!" Employees felt that since I was working to hold their boss accountable, telling me about their woes was perhaps their best and only shot for some real change!

Over time, I have found the same principles of success apply to both groups, even though their perspectives are very different. While entrepreneurs live in a world of calculated risk for calculated reward, most employees seek security and steady advancement. This isn't to say that each group seeks a different destination, only different pathways to that destination.

Unexpectedly, the friction between these two methods of work-life goal attainment lends itself to success in businesses of all sizes. The resulting pressure between entrepreneurial grand vision and employee attention to detail can lead to great progress. Unfortunately, characteristic of friction, the differences also create a lot of heat. All too often, the path of the business leader and the path of the employee not only intersect but also collide.

The message of *Invaluable* isn't to remove the friction but to contain the heat. While heat left uncontained causes chaos, channeled and focused heat will generate a lot of lift and momentum. Channeled, focused heat propels rockets into space. Similarly, when both business leaders and employees understand each other, even though their differences in perspective remain, they are better equipped to find ways to work together.

They begin to realize they share the same end goals. Business owners and employees realize that, at least in matters of business success and even the economy, they are in it together.

So, here's to reaching new heights—together.

FRICTION

Jason could sense her behind him . . . hovering.

Through nearly six months of internship and a couple more months on the job, he had developed a sixth sense—his "Tracy-dar." He could feel her coming a mile away.

He didn't need to see her face to know she was rolling her eyes. He didn't need to listen beyond the soft hum of his computer to hear her stifled sigh. He didn't even need to have his feet on the floor to know she was tapping her foot impatiently.

"Yes, Tracy?" he asked, his eyes never leaving the computer screen.

Tracy now sighed audibly. "Where is that research report on next quarter's trends?"

Jason barely masked his frustration. He spoke quickly, so as to not give her a chance to interrupt. "It's coming. I should have it to you by Friday. You asked me to start working on the sales projections yesterday. You said those were urgent. I assumed that meant they went to the top of my stack. So I've been working on getting those ready. It's what you asked me to do."

"Well, that's what happens when you assume," she chided. "When I told you the sales projections were urgent, that didn't mean I wanted you to stop working on the trend report. I still expected you to get that to me this morning."

How was I supposed to know that? Is ESP part of my job description now? Jason thought. But what he said was, "Okay. . . ."

"This is why you're paid a salary now, Jason," Tracy continued. "You're supposed to work the hours it takes to get these things done. You may have punched a time clock when you were an intern, but now GreenGarb expects more from you."

Yeah, that's why I came here out of college, to get minimum-wage pay for a never-ending workweek. Jason spun in his chair and gave a quick salute. "Okay, boss. I'll get right on it."

"So, when can I get the trend report?"

Jason looked around at the papers strewn around his cubicle. "Uh . . . well, I guess if I stop working on the sales projections right now, I could get it to you by the end of the day. Good enough?"

Tracy frowned. "It'll have to be, I guess." She paused for a moment as if to say something else to Jason, then turned and walked back toward her office.

Jason clenched his fists in frustration behind Tracy's back and sighed. "Looks like another long day again. This is not why I went to college," he muttered to himself. Resigned to his current fate, he turned back to the computer and began pulling up the trend report, again.

FRUSTRATION

Jason absently tapped out a rhythm on his steering wheel as he sped along I-11. The radio blared a familiar tune, but he wasn't listening.

Am I burned out already? Jason wondered to himself. *What a wimp. Snap out of it!*

Jason felt he had a solid work ethic. He had never considered himself a privileged kid and had learned the value of hard work growing up with his family's small business. Although he hadn't been a star athlete in high school, he had also learned teamwork and discipline from a tough basketball coach.

In college it had been much the same. He did the assignments, put in enough effort to get decent grades, and even had a little time to goof around with friends and date. Overall, he always did what his teachers expected him to do and graduated with a respectable GPA.

In his business classes the teachers had warned him to expect long hours early on—that junior employees in almost any business were expected to pay their dues. So, after graduation, when GreenGarb had offered him a marketing assistant position following his internship, he felt he knew what to expect. He knew Tracy was very smart and talented, albeit a little authoritarian and neglectful at times. He had seen the long hours other employees put in. Early on in his internship, he had even seen the CEO, Helen, put in long hours—though he had seen less of that lately. Although this was his first job out of school, from his parents' business he knew it took an incredible amount of work to keep a company competitive.

Then why am I so upset?

He knew deep down it wasn't about the hours, even though he was spending more time than he liked at GreenGarb. It was about the feeling of being underappreciated and undervalued. Tracy treated him like a grunt. She barely acknowledged his effort, let alone that he was a human being. When he performed the tasks she asked him to do, his efforts weren't recognized. When he showed initiative and tried to give his input for improvement or make a recommendation, Tracy *acted* as if she cared about his opinion, but she really did nothing about it. And often he felt attacked for mistakes he didn't even realize he was making, like today when he didn't get the trend report in on the date and time Tracy expected.

What frustrated him most of all, though, was that he knew if he were in Tracy's position, he could do a whole lot better.

He sighed as he flipped on the turn signal to move toward the next exit. Jason had learned one thing over the twenty-two years of his life—whenever he was confused or upset, there was one person he could always depend on to pick him up and point him in the right direction.

He was going to see Charlie.

PERSPECTIVE

Jason pulled into the parking lot of Palm Terrace Community. Grabbing the keys, he jumped out of his small car. He felt the warmth of the setting sun on his face as he jogged down the palm-lined walkway. As he reached the door, he smiled to himself. Things always seemed better around Charlie.

He waved to the head nurse, Nancy, who called out, "Hey, Jason, when are you going to let me set you up with my niece?"

Jason winked as he walked by. "Your niece? You know *you're* the only one for me, Nancy."

"Charmer!" She laughed and shushed him with her hands. "I think Charlie is back in his room. It's Thursday."

"John Wayne night, of course. Thanks, Nancy."

Jason nodded to familiar elderly faces as he walked back through the residence halls of Palm Terrace. An occasional "Hello, Jason" and "Good to see you, son" greeted him as he passed by.

Walking up to the slightly cracked door of room 134, he could hear the familiar voice of the Duke drifting around the corner. "*You wanna quit, quit! Go back to the bottle, get drunk. One thing, though. The next time someone throws a dollar into a spittoon—*"

"'Don't expect me to do anything about it! Just get down on your knees and get it.'" Jason recited with a grin as he opened the door.

Charles Fullman, a wiry, weathered oak of a man, nearly ninety years old, smiled widely and began to push himself up from the easy chair. "Jason, my boy! It's so good to see you!"

Jason rested a hand on Charlie's shoulder. "No need to get up." But Jason felt Charlie's deceptive strength surge as he rose from the chair and stood eye to eye with him.

"Nonsense!" Charlie laughed and clapped Jason firmly on the shoulders with large, gnarled hands. "It's always an honor to see my favorite grandson. Have a seat and let's talk." He reached down slowly to the remote and pressed the off button for the TV.

"I didn't mean to interrupt the Duke," Jason said as he sat down on an ancient sofa. He fondly remembered many Thursday evenings as a boy watching and memorizing every John Wayne film with Charlie. After Jason's grandmother passed away, his grandfather had built a small house on the lot across the street from their family, so Jason had visited often.

The one thing Jason never did was call him grandpa. Charlie would never allow it.

"The Duke can wait!" Charlie nodded firmly as if making a proclamation. He grinned, his eyes twinkling as he looked at Jason. "Tell me about your day. Have you conquered the world yet?"

Jason smiled ruefully. "My day was okay. Let's not talk about it. How is Palm Terrace treating you?"

Charlie paused for a moment as if to say something, but thought better of it. Instead, he replied, "Great. Great! There're a few fellows here who like to play chess, too. We get together every few days or so and brawl. John is a damn fine player, but I'd never tell him. That son of a sow's head is already big enough as it is!" He laughed loudly.

Jason had become used to Charlie's colorful vocabulary, a carryover from his Navy days in World War II. The skill at chess was also something Charlie had picked up in the course of the war to fight off boredom during the long stretches of downtime at sea. Jason knew from the bits and pieces of what his dad told him that Charlie had done some heroic things during the war and had been decorated a couple of times. However, he had learned not to ask his grandfather about the war. It just wasn't something Charlie cared to talk about.

"I hope you let them win—occasionally," Jason said. "You used to let me win when I was a kid, didn't you?"

"Gotta keep 'em encouraged. Gotta let 'em think they've got a chance." Charlie winked. He did that—winking—a lot, Jason had noticed. "Although, I didn't let you win as much as you might think. You were always a fast one. Even faster than your older brothers and your sister, if I remember right."

"I had to be fast or I never would have been able to eat at meals!" Competing with three older brothers and an older sister had been a way of life for Jason.

"True, true," Charlie nodded. Then he looked Jason squarely in the eyes. "Out with it, Jason. Tell me about your work. What's going on?"

Jason sighed. "Ah . . . well, okay. Here it is: I think I hate my job." Charlie smiled knowingly, and Jason continued. "I know, I know. I just got started. All jobs are hard. I should stick to it. When you were a boy things were different. I know I should be more patient—but it's just not working out."

Charlie raised his ponderous eyebrows. "You're already defensive? You don't even know what I was going to say."

"Sorry."

"No apology necessary." Charlie chuckled. "But when I was a boy, things *were* different."

"I know, and I respect that. I mean, you were drafted into World War II. You grew up during the Depression. Your generation worked harder than kids like me ever had to. I respect that. Really, I do. A lot. It's just that. . . . "

"Just that, what?"

Jason shifted uncomfortably in his chair. He had always been able to speak his mind with his grand-father, just as he would to a friend. Jason wasn't worried about offending Charlie; he just didn't want to let him down. Charlie always expected great things of his grandson, and told him so often.

"I guess I just expected more from this job. I thought I'd get more respect. I graduated with a good GPA. I did well in all my classes. I'm not dumb. Yet they've got me doing pretty minor stuff. I'm capable of a lot more, but they won't give me the chance. I make suggestions to my boss but she treats me like a teenager."

Charlie sat attentively, waiting for his grandson to continue.

"I guess I'm thinking of quitting."

Charlie replied, "Quit your job? Why? Didn't you just get that job?"

Jason said, "I've been there for at least six weeks; almost seven months if you count my internship." Charlie just smiled, and Jason corrected himself. "Well, you're right. I guess it hasn't been that long, has it?" More to himself than to Charlie, he said, "It just seems a lot longer."

"Well, I know that feeling!" Charlie boomed. "I think I felt that at least once a week in the service." He stopped and added, "But rarely with a job. I always enjoyed good, honest work of any kind. I suppose I was grateful just to have a job at your age." He held up a hand in consolation. "But I do know it's different today. A young man like you has all sorts of options, especially in today's world. You don't have a family to feed yet. You don't have to tie yourself down . . . not yet, at least. So let's imagine you did something else for a job. What else would you do?"

Jason threw up his hands. "That's just it—nothing! I can't think of what else I would do! I mean, I really love marketing. I like the idea of figuring out ways to reach people. I even like the product I'm selling. I believe in it. It's a good company. But maybe there is another opportunity somewhere else. I could start looking for a job elsewhere."

Charlie held up a hand. "Wait a moment, Jason. If you love what you do, and you like the company, why would you look anywhere else? You've already built up some steam at this company. Seems like you're trying to jump off a horse that's moving onto another horse that's standing still. You do that and you're likely to fall flat on your butt."

Jason chuckled. "Not something the Duke would do, huh?"

"No, sir," Charlie said firmly. "No–he–wouldn't." He rapped his knuckles on the wooden arms of his chair to emphasize each word. "What he would do is stay in there until the job gets done. And it's what I know you have done your whole life, Jason."

Sometimes, Jason told himself. He almost believed those things about him were true when Charlie said them the way he did. *Almost.*

INVALUABLE

Charlie continued, "I never once looked for a job in my life, you know. They always came to me. I knew that even if I didn't like everything about a job, if I made myself invaluable, sooner or later someone would take notice and a new opportunity would come."

"Invaluable? What do you mean?" Jason asked.

"I mean irreplaceable, Jason. Someone your company can't live without. A top producer. The go-to guy. Different. *Invaluable!*" Charlie said the last word more forcefully this time, as if the word itself explained everything.

Jason was settling into his normal comfort level with his grandfather and started to open up. "Sorry, Charlie. I'm not buying it," he grumbled. "The only way I could make myself invaluable is if I was the boss. And that's not happening anytime soon. You know I respect you, but that's just not practical in today's world. We're all just boxes of information and activity that get traded around. The faster things get, the more technology there is out there, and the less valuable humans become. We're more and more just computers that get upgraded or discarded. No one keeps their job for more than a couple of years now, anyway."

Charlie sat a bit straighter in his chair, and leaned forward. Jason recognized his grandfather's "teaching" position. "Forget being invaluable for a moment. Let's say you're going to stick in with this job, Jason. Let's imagine quitting isn't an option— even though it is. What are two things that would need to change for you to love this job?"

Jason thought for a moment and then said, "I guess I would need to make more money. If I had more money then I'd feel a lot better about the hours I am putting in and I could put up with a lot more crap."

Charlie smiled. "Of course, of course. But even if they paid you more, that wouldn't be enough, would it? You've only given me one thing. What else would need to change in order for you to love your job?"

Jason sighed. "Respect. I need more respect . . . well, not just respect, but authority as well. I guess I just want people to treat me like I'm making a difference and my opinion matters. What do you call that?"

Charlie nodded. "*Respect* is a fine word." He then leaned farther forward in his chair and looked intently at his grandson. For a moment, Jason caught a glimpse of a man thirty years younger. Charlie asked, "What have you done to merit that change?"

"Merit the change? What do you mean?"

"I want to show you something." Charlie began to rise from his chair with difficulty. Jason started to get up to help him and Charlie barked, "Sit down. Sit down. I'm not ready for a nursemaid yet." Charlie finished standing and walked steadily over to the bookshelf. "Where is that one? 'Forty-eight through fifty' . . . here it is." He pulled out an old red cloth-covered photo album, still in good shape except for a generous layer of dust. Charlie carefully wiped the cover and blew on it for good measure. "Scoot over, boy."

Jason slid over as Charlie eased himself carefully onto the sofa. Then he began thumbing through the pages slowly, mumbling to himself. "Where is that one?" Finally, he pointed to a picture midway through the album. "Here it is, Jason. Look at this."

Charlie was pointing to a black-and-white photo of a group of ordinary, hard-working men standing in front of what looked to be a sawmill. It was one of those "old photos" that Jason had seen many times as a boy. He had never really noticed anything special about these photos before, and saw nothing unusual in this one, other than that his grandfather appeared a whole lot younger and even more wiry than he was now.

"When I came back from the war, the best job I could find was in the local lumber mill. They paid me about ninety cents an hour working long days six days a week. It was hard work, but that was good money. Now don't look at me like that, Jason. I'm not going to lecture you about 'when I was a boy'!" Jason muttered an apology and Charlie continued. "I say it was good money, but it wasn't good enough for me. I wanted more. I was always thinking of ways I could get paid more for doing less. Maybe we know where you get that from, hmm?"

Jason smiled. People had told him many times growing up that he resembled his grandfather even more than his mom or dad.

"Well, anyway, I wanted more, but I was grateful for what I had in the moment. There was an old Master Chief I knew in the war—Pond was his name—who taught me to focus on the job at hand and make sure I was doing it right before I looked for more. He was a bible-loving man and always quoted 1 Samuel 15:22 to me. I got tired of hearing that blasted scripture!"

Jason looked puzzled, so Charlie, in a sanctimonious voice Jason guessed must be an impression of Master Chief Pond, recited, "'To obey is better than sacrifice.'"

"What does that have to do with my job?"

"It means you better make sure you're taking care of what you're supposed to be doing before you worry about doing something new! No one cares about how good you are at building a ship if you didn't clean the mess hall like you were supposed to."

"Got it," Jason said.

Charlie continued, "So I decided I first needed to learn all I could about the job I had. I asked a lot of questions of fellows who had worked the mill longer than I had. I learned my position, Jason."

"That's why I went to college," Jason said. "To get a good job."

Charlie chuckled and nodded. "And that was a good thing. I never was able to complete my degree and I'm glad you were able to do it. But may I suggest something? You went to college to learn about your industry. You went to learn about marketing, and how to be an intelligent and well-rounded thinker. But what you didn't learn is how to work in your *position*. Companies make positions; the market makes positions; not colleges."

"I'm not sure I get what you're saying. What's the difference?"

"The difference, Jason, is that every company *is* different. There was more than one lumber mill where I lived, but I wasn't working for all of them. Just one. That one. And I wasn't filling all the positions in the company. Just one. I had to learn how to be an expert at that one position, in that one company.

"I was working with the crew on the large saw blade, and it had its own temperament. I had to learn everything there was to know about that blade from people who had been there before me. Not only that, but my boss had his own temperament." Charlie pointed to a man in the picture with a powerful frame and a square jaw covered with stubble. "I had to learn everything there was to know about him, from people who had worked for him before me. Really, I had to learn how to be careful around both him and his saw to keep from getting my hand cut off!" He held up a wide, calloused hand for emphasis.

"Okay, I'm with you, Charlie. But what does that have to do with becoming invaluable?"

"Everything." Charlie grinned. "It didn't take more than a few months for my boss to realize I wasn't making as many mistakes as everyone else. And I was keeping things moving . . . not too fast, mind you, but fast enough. Soon I had a reputation for being someone who didn't make mistakes. I was different. Invaluable.

"Now, my boss didn't like that occasionally I got a little more time off than the others. He also probably wished I had kept my mouth shut more often than I did—"

"Really?" Jason feigned shock.

"Watch yourself," Charlie said in mock menace and then continued, "but he couldn't argue with the results. So he gave me the occasional raise and let me have some perks the others didn't get . . . because I was invaluable to the company. Others could have come in and done my job, but no one could do it as well."

"So being invaluable is just about doing your job better than everyone else?" Jason asked. "Then you get away with whatever you want? That sounds simplistic to me."

Charlie nodded knowingly. "It would be, son, if that's all there was to it. But being invaluable means a lot more than that. I didn't really stumble across the formula until a few years later, though, when I'd moved into a sales position."

Jason was a bit surprised. He knew his grandfather had worked for a lumber mill, but didn't know he had been in sales. "What do you mean sales position, Charlie? I didn't know you worked in sales."

Charlie nodded his head. "Yes, for several years I worked in sales. I was moving large bundles of timber to various commercial builders around the country. That's what gave me enough money to fund my first business."

"I never knew that," Jason said. "Sorry to interrupt. So, what's the formula?"

Charlie cleared his throat and continued. "Well, my sales manager at the lumber mill was also the business owner, Mr. Bevels." Charlie pointed to a middle-aged man in the middle of the lumber mill photo. "It wasn't a very large company and Mr. Bevels wanted me to take over the job he had been doing. You see, he had been the one doing all the sales for the company. He was getting a bit tired of doing too many things at once. I guess he saw that I was a good worker and decided to hand it off to me. He liked the way I worked. I suppose he saw that I had the potential to do sales."

Jason raised his eyebrows. "I'm confused. You mean he saw that you would be a good sales rep from your doing good work on the lumber mill floor?"

Charlie considered Jason's question with a small smile of surprise. "I never really thought about it before. That doesn't make much sense, does it? But for some reason, that's how it happened for me. He knew I was young and had potential. He saw that I was thinking ahead and solving problems." Charlie scratched at his grizzled afternoon shadow absent-mindedly. "I guess what he really saw was that I was a good communicator. He said

I spent a lot of time talking to other people on the floor, and I was able to convince my boss to give me time off." He chuckled to himself. "I guess he figured if I could sell to that guy, I could sell to anybody else."

Jason smiled and Charlie continued, "So anyway, my new boss, Mr. Bevels, taught me something very important on my first day on the job. It's always stayed with me. He said, 'Charlie, you can make as much money as you want. But make no mistake—I'm not the one who's going to pay it to you. If you want a raise, go talk to the market, not me.'"

Jason chewed on that for a moment. "So he told you how much money you made was dependent on how well you sold? That's a bit obvious, isn't it?"

Charlie smiled. "It might seem like that. However, I heard him say the same thing to his managers—people who had nothing to do with sales. I also noticed my income was increasing the better I got at sales, not just because my commissions were going up, but because more opportunities seemed to show up at my door. I was able to take advantage of all those opportunities. I was starting to get better and better at my job. But still, it took me awhile to figure out what old Mr. Bevels was saying. In fact, I don't think I really figured it out until many years later. I was listening to this radio program hosted by a man named Earl Nightingale. Have you heard of him?"

"Yes, I think so," Jason said. "Wasn't he some sort of motivational speaker?"

Charlie chuckled. "I suppose you could say that. Anyway, what I heard him say really put what Mr. Bevels said into a formula for the first time. This is what I heard Earl say:

"'The amount of money you make will always be in direct proportion to: number one, the demand for what you do; number two, your ability to do it; and number three, the difficulty of replacing you.'

"That's it." Charlie nodded his head as if that was all there was to say. "That's the formula."

"That sounds pretty basic," Jason said.

"Son, when you've been around as long as I have, you realize after a while that it's *all* basic." He chuckled. "We're the ones who like to make it more complicated than it really is."

The formula seemed overly simplistic to Jason, but his grandfather was someone he respected so he said, "Can you hold on just a moment? I want to send myself an e-mail so I don't forget that." Jason pulled out his phone and typed three words:

```
Demand
Ability
Irreplaceability
```

His grandfather shook his head and mumbled to himself, laughing quietly. Jason didn't have to ask. He knew that laugh was his grandfather's way of saying, "I can't believe the things you can do nowadays." After he hit the send button, Jason looked at his grandfather and said, "So, what did you do after you heard that on the radio? Were you able to increase how much money you made and the amount of respect you got at the lumber mill?"

Charlie smiled. "Well, remember, I didn't hear that bit from Earl Nightingale until much later. So early on, all I had to go on was what Mr. Bevels told me: 'If you want a raise, go talk to the market, not me.' I realize now that I didn't have much control over what the market was willing to pay—at least I didn't think so at the time. All I could really control was the job I did and how good I was doing the job. I think that's

28

what Mr. Nightingale meant when he said, 'your ability to do it and the difficulty of replacing you.'

"Well, I set about trying to become the best salesman Mr. Bevels had ever had." Charlie laughed at that thought. "I guess it wasn't hard, because the only salesman Mr. Bevels had ever had—was Mr. Bevels!" Charlie laughed even louder, and Jason just shook his head at him as Charlie's laugh turned into a bit of a coughing fit. "But that wasn't it, exactly," Charlie continued. "I wasn't trying to be just better than Mr. Bevels. I was trying to be the best damn salesman in the world—at least when it came to selling lumber. For me, it wasn't enough to be good. I had to become the best. I had to learn my job the same way I learned how to run the big saw and work with my boss in the mill. I had to learn how to deal with my customers. I had to learn the art of being a salesman. And I had to learn the art of being a salesman within Bevels and Company."

"So what you're telling me, Charlie, is I need to begin viewing my job like an art form? Right?"

Charlie shook his head gently. "I think you know me well enough to know I'm not telling you to do anything. In fact, I think you probably would've figured this out without coming in and talking to me. I think you probably knew this before you came here. All I really suggest is that you answer this question: 'Are you invaluable or are you easily replaceable?' Once you figure that out, I think you'll solve this on your own. You'll figure out the right path yourself.

"You know a whole lot more about this world and your job than I could ever hope to know." Charlie shook his head in disbelief. "I still don't quite understand how you can pick up that little phone of yours there and send yourself a memo. The tools you have now are fantastic, compared to what I had to work with. And the knowledge you gained in college is valuable," Jason began to make a wisecrack but Charlie continued, "even if you may not feel like it gave you what you want right now. Maybe even just getting your college degree made you more valuable to the market. But now it's time to continue your education and take the next step."

Jason grinned slyly. "So, Professor, what is the next step I should take?"

Charlie replied, "Again, just answer this question: are you invaluable or are you replaceable?"

"Wow, I wouldn't even know how to answer that."

"Let's make up a way of answering it. Let's say there's a scale—one to ten. One is completely replaceable and ten is invaluable. Take a stab at it. What's your best guess?"

Jason grimaced and sighed, deep in thought. "If I had to take a wild guess at it, I guess I would say I'm right in the middle. I don't know, what do you think?"

Charlie laughed to himself. "Now, how would I answer that? I'm not your boss, am I? We'll just call it a 'five' for now and see where it goes from there."

"Okay, so I'm a five," Jason said reservedly. "I guess that stinks. Now what?"

"Now," Charlie said, raising his voice as if he were about to deliver a sermon. "Stop doing less valuable activities. That's what I did. After I heard Earl's comment, I realized the only thing I really had any control of was what I could do and how hard it was to replace me. Sure, market demand had an effect on how much I would get paid, and a few times over the years I had to change jobs because the demand for those jobs changed or even disappeared. But really all it came down to was my ability to focus what I was doing on my most valuable activities. My most valuable activities were the things I did that had the most value in the marketplace. And when I spent time on those activities the amount of money I made really increased." Charlie slowly got up from the couch and put the photo album back on the shelf as he said, "When you focus on your most valuable activities, both your ability and the difficulty of replacing you are increased."

Jason felt a bit confused. *This certainly isn't something they taught me in college,* he thought. "I'm not sure I know what you mean. Are you telling me I should switch jobs so I can find the one that pays the most?"

"Well," Charlie replied, "It may come to that, but not yet, I think. Jason, they have you doing a lot of different things at that company you work for, right?"

"Yeah, a *lot* of things. Sometimes I feel like I'm just an intern still . . . running around doing all the errands no one else wants to do."

As Charlie moved back to the couch, he pointed at Jason as if he had just said something profound. "That's it! The question you need to answer is, of all those errands they have you doing, which are really making an impact on the company's bottom line? Which of them are increasing the amount of money the business owner or the shareholders are making? I say that because ultimately how much money *they* make governs how much you make."

"Not always," Jason said.

"More than you realize," Charlie replied. "But that's not the real point. Of the tasks that you do, which tasks are just wasting time? Which tasks are just busywork that some manager is giving you because they see you sitting around? And which tasks have real meaning? Figure out the answer to this and you'll figure out a way to get the money you want to make and the respect you feel you deserve."

Jason shook his head. "I don't know the answer to that question. I'm not sure I know where to begin or even if Tracy wants me to begin figuring it out."

Charlie gave his grandson an encouraging slap on the knee. "Don't answer it now. Don't even try to answer it now. Take some time with it. You may even want to ask that manager of yours what she thinks. I bet she'll have some good answers for you." Charlie sighed. "Did that help you, Jason, or did I just ramble on too much? I am an old man, you know. Sometimes I do that," Charlie said as he winked at Jason.

"I think it helped. I'll get back to you on it." Jason yawned. "Do you know what I really need right now, though?"

"Some sleep?"

"A little *Rio Bravo*," Jason said, smiling.

"I thought you'd never ask. . . ."

MANAGER

```
Demand
Ability
Irreplaceability
```

Jason stared at his computer screen and the e-mail he had sent himself the night before. The conversation with his grandfather played through his head.

Jason was lost in thought as he heard a voice behind him.

"I haven't checked my e-mail yet this morning. Were you able to get that report to me?"

"Yeah," Jason muttered.

"Great. I'll go check it out right now. What are you working on next?"

"Nothing," Jason said absentmindedly. Tracy was about to make a comment, likely regarding Jason's laziness, when Jason interrupted her. "Tracy, am I invaluable?"

"Well, right now, in this moment, if you're not doing anything, you're not valuable at all," she snickered. "If you were to get back to work, then you'd be really valuable to me. We've got this project going on—"

"Of all the things I do at work, then," Jason interrupted, "which is the most valuable?" Tracy appeared stunned for a moment, so he continued, "You've got me doing all sorts of things, but which of those things really make a difference in the company?"

Tracy tilted her head to the side for a moment and thought. Finally, she said, "those that have the greatest impact on our customer."

"Like what? This is a marketing team, so what work activities do we perform that have the greatest impact on our customer? We're just trying to bring people through the door, right?"

"Well," Tracy said slowly, "for our department it's important for us to put together good marketing strategies that get us in contact with new customers. Things like developing our ad strategy, coming up with new methods of reaching new customers, developing color schemes and brand imagery. I would also say coordinating with vendors. What are you getting at, Jason?"

Tracy was beginning to appear perturbed so Jason held up his hands in surrender. "Stick with me for just a moment, Tracy. I don't want to waste your time. I'm really trying to figure something out here, so I'd appreciate your help."

"Okay."

"All the things you just mentioned are things you are currently doing, Tracy. This is an established company, so you already had a lot of those things under control before I even got here. I'm just an assistant, and those kinds of decisions are ones you are making as marketing director. So, my question is, what is it that *I* do that helps you accomplish those things? What is it that *I* do that is most valuable to this department?"

Tracy sighed, grabbed a chair from a nearby cubicle, and sat down next to Jason. "Well, you're doing the nuts and bolts of that stuff. Yeah, I may be looking at the bigger picture, but I'm asking you to help put the projects into action and make sure they take place. When you execute those directions, or management's larger directives, well, that's where you're valuable to me. That's where you're helping the company the most. And as a company, we need you to stay in sync with what we ultimately agreed upon."

She gave Jason a sidelong glance and cautiously continued, "What are you searching for here? It looks like you're trying to get a particular answer."

"Maybe, maybe not."

"Let me ask you something, then," Tracy said. "A moment ago you mentioned the word *invaluable*. What do *you* think makes you invaluable?"

"Well, I don't know, really." Jason found himself a bit surprised for a moment. This was one of the longest conversations he'd ever had with Tracy. Carefully, he continued, "Last night I was talking to my grandpa, Charlie. He said I need to become invaluable if I'm going to like my job . . . more." He inserted the last word quickly, hoping she didn't catch the pause.

"You don't like your job?" Tracy interjected.

"Most of the time I do," Jason lied. "Anyway, he told me I needed to figure out what my most valuable activities are. He also told me the best place to start figuring that out was to ask you. So I'm asking you."

Tracy briefly appeared shocked and then covered it up with a smile. "Well, that's good of your grandfather to do that. So, let me be the manager that I like to be." *What kind of manager is* that? Jason thought as Tracy continued, "I'll ask you, instead: What do you think it is that makes you most valuable here? Out of all the things you do, what do you think it is that makes you invaluable to this company?"

"Oh, I get it. So you take the same question I asked you and you ask it back to me, huh?" He smiled amiably but suppressed the urge to roll his eyes.

"Absolutely, and I'll tell you why, Jason. Because this is what I *should* be doing to help you become better—or invaluable—to the company. Helen has been telling us we need to work on doing a better job of training our teams, not just telling them what to do."

Jason had seen an e-mail or two from the CEO encouraging the managers to begin meeting with their employees regularly and provide training, but he had ignored it as not relevant to his job. He had become used to ignoring "little details" like that over the last few months, mostly because Tracy never paid attention to them either.

Tracy echoed his thoughts. "I've been so wrapped up in all the different projects and initiatives we have going on that I've really neglected doing that sort of thing. So I think it's a great question. It's one I haven't thought of before. I appreciate your grandpa— Charlie, you said his name was?—sharing it.

"So now that you brought it up, let's run with it. And let's start by having me give you the assignment to answer that question. What is it that you do here that makes you invaluable? What separates you from all the other employees we have here? Why don't you think about it and we can talk about it later."

Tracy didn't appear to want to get the answer right then. Jason, however, had learned that he needed to talk to Tracy when he had the opportunity or he might never have the chance again. So he jumped in. "Well, Charlie said it really came down to three things." He pointed to the monitor to show Tracy the e-mail he was looking at. "One is demand for something, another is my ability to do it, and the other is the difficulty of replacing me. But he also said I don't have much control over demand other than the career I choose. So I guess my most valuable activities are the things I'm really good at and the things you would have a hard time replacing. So, I guess I have to figure out what it is I'm good at . . ."

"Yes," Tracy prompted.

"And I'll have to figure out the things I do better than someone else. Well, at least the things that would be hard for you to replace."

"If you were to make a chart for that, say, a simple spreadsheet, how would it look?" Tracy asked.

Jason grabbed a piece of paper and thought for a moment. He shrugged and said, "I guess I don't have to make this too complex, right?" Tracy nodded and he began to write:

Activity	Strength?	Hard to Replace?

"Could you turn that into a spreadsheet and send it to me? I'd like to try filling it out myself." Tracy pulled out her phone. "I'll tell you what. Let's do this right and schedule a meeting—the way that consultant, Phil, told us to. Let's find a time when we can compare answers when I'm not feeling rushed by the project. Do you have your calendar open?"

MVAs

Jason sat in a chair in Tracy's modest office. He had been waiting several minutes already, not surprised that Tracy was late for their meeting. She was always late.

The door flew open and Tracy stepped in, shutting it quickly behind her. "Sorry I'm late. I was held up in the last meeting. But I'm here. Let's get going. Did you find out what your strengths are?" She rushed to her desk and sat down. She quickly organized papers that were out of place on her desk and then looked at Jason intently. *She's trying a little too hard,* Jason thought smugly. *She's trying to make up for being late by showing me what a good manager she is.*

Jason pushed a printout across the desk and into her hands. On it was the following:

Jason's Chart

Activity	Strength?	Hard to Replace?
Market research—internet		
Writing reports	X	
Coordinating focus groups		
Running errands		
Managing Tracy's schedule	X	
Fielding calls from vendors	X	
Designing materials	X	
Copywriting	X	X
Answering e-mail, voicemail, and so on	X	

Note: For an advanced version of this exercise and step-by-step instructions, see the Appendix.

"As you can see, I had a problem with the 'hard-to-replace' part," Jason said. "Honestly, I felt like most everything I do would be pretty easy to replace. The only one I could come up with was copywriting, since you and others here at the company have been training me for months about the 'GreenGarb way' of saying things."

Tracy shook her head. "I disagree. I look at this list and see at least two more activities I would have a hard time replacing. One is managing my schedule. I had someone do that before and they screwed everything up. You're actually very organized and understand my schedule very well. It'd take me months to train someone to do that right again."

"Okay," Jason said, as he scribbled a check mark in that row.

"Also, you're very talented at design. I would say some of the things you put together look better than even what I do. So check that one, as well."

While Jason did so, Tracy said, "I have mine on my computer. Let me print it out." She hit a few keys on the keyboard and the printer began humming dutifully. She handed the result to Jason:

Tracy's Chart

Activity	Strength?	Hard to Replace?
Coordinate with VPs	X	X
Discuss campaigns with Helen (CEO)	X	X
Budgeting		
Work on marketing materials		X
Approve marketing materials		X
Write and submit new marketing strategies	X	X

(Continued)

45

Tracy's chart (Continued)

Networking, develop strategic partners	X	X
Scheduling		
Respond to e-mail and phone calls		X
Conduct focus groups	X	X
Update company blog	X	X
Monitor social networks regarding company		
Train team	X	X
Travel to events	N/A	X

"This list is twice as long as mine!" Jason said. "You sure have a lot to do."

"Well, it's a small but growing company," Tracy said. "We really can't hire people to do each little thing, so it just all falls on me, I guess." Jason stared intently at Tracy's list and then set his and hers side by side.

"What do you see?" Tracy asked.

"I'm not sure," Jason said. "It seems to me like there is some overlap here. I mean, it's not obvious. Not everything lines up perfectly, but I see places where I could be helping you better. Especially between my strengths and your weak—" Jason caught himself. "Uh, what do we want to call them?"

"No need to be diplomatic," Tracy laughed. "They're my weaknesses. I know I'm deficient when it comes to organization. That's why I hand off some of my scheduling to you."

"Maybe you could do more of that? I mean, I'm actually pretty good at being organized and keeping on top of schedules. Maybe you could let me handle your schedule completely?" Jason hesitated for a moment, then decided to be a bit bolder. "Maybe if I did that for you, you wouldn't always show up late for meetings."

Tracy smiled ruefully. "I'm not always late, you know." Jason raised his eyebrows. "Okay, maybe once or twice in my lifetime I've showed up on time. I suppose I haven't really recognized your ability as well as I should have before. I guess it's just a little scary giving up that much responsibility to someone else."

"You mean like when Helen stopped doing all the marketing stuff herself and hired you?" Jason jumped in, now feeling a bit more confident he could be direct with Tracy without offending her.

Tracy stopped and nodded. "Yes, you're right. I've heard her talk about that before, too. She said one of the hardest things she ever had to do as a business owner was give up control to someone else and delegate responsibility. I guess I thought that was a challenge only for a company's founder. It's just . . ."

"Just what?" Jason prodded.

"Well, if someone starts doing the business owner's job for her, that's called retirement. If someone starts doing my job for *me,* as a manager, that's called unemployment." The two sat in silence for a moment. Then Tracy continued, "But I guess that's what your grandpa Charlie meant by focusing on your 'most valuable' activities. We're not talking about your doing my job for me. We're only talking about you doing the things for me that I'm not very good at—well, stink at!—so that I can spend more time on the things I'm very good at."

"'Stop doing less valuable activities,'" Jason interjected. "That's what he said."

"What?"

"That's what Charlie said to me when I asked him what I should do. I said I was about a 'five' on the invaluable scale, and he told me to 'stop doing less valuable activities.'"

"Your grandpa sounds like a very smart man," Tracy said. "I'll have to meet him someday. Sounds like you and I need to spend some time working on a plan for how I can get my calendar, and maybe even some of my e-mail, off my plate."

Jason was surprised. Here was his boss telling him he was going to have more to do, maybe a lot more to do, yet it felt like a burden was lifting off his shoulders. *Maybe it's because I don't feel like so much of a grunt, now,* he thought. *I can actually contribute instead of feeling like a "go-fer" for once.* "Yeah, let's work on that. I've already got some ideas. One thing still puzzles me, though. I can help you by using some of my strengths to 'fill in' your weaknesses. But what about me?"

"What do you mean?" Tracy asked.

"Well, what about my weaknesses? Not only do I hate doing market research, coordinating focus groups, and running errands, but they're not even that valuable! Who do I give those to so I can focus on my strengths?"

"I see," Tracy said thoughtfully, then grinned. "Where do you think you could remove some of those from your schedule?"

This time, Jason did roll his eyes—but with a teasing smile. "There you go again, answering my question with a question. Well, you did tell me a few weeks ago that we have another intern—I mean a *new* intern—Candice. You mentioned before I could start giving her some of my workload."

"I do remember telling you about the intern." Tracy paused and then asked slyly, "So, what was in the way of your using her before?"

Jason shrugged. "A combination of things, I guess. For one, maybe it's that same fear of giving someone else my job. Also, I didn't really know what I could or should give her to do before we had this conversation. For another reason, I guess I . . ."

"What?"

"Well," Jason gulped. "I guess I didn't know whether to take you seriously when you said it. You sometimes say stuff like that and then later forget you said it or contradict yourself." He held his breath, waiting to see if he had said too much.

Tracy frowned. "I don't know if that's really true, Jason. You need to give me a little more credit. But I do admit I have so many things going on that I'm not always paying close attention to what I'm saying. I'll try to be more careful from now on. If you have a question, just ask me about it. And I'll try to make sure we have these 'huddles' more often in the future to make sure we're on the same page.

"But, in short, yes, you can start delegating some of those tasks on your list to Candice."

"Hmmm. Is there a problem with this?" Jason asked. "Do we just keep delegating all the less valuable work down the line? Who ends up actually doing the work no one wants to do?"

"I think the maxim 'one person's trash is another person's treasure' applies here. Remember, we're not getting rid of everything—just the activities that are less valuable for *us*. For me, it's a less valuable activity to spend time coordinating calendars and screening calls. However, for you it becomes an MVA—" She laughed. "I just made that up. Like it?"

"MVA is Most Valuable Activity?"

"Right . . . anyway, for you it's an MVA to do those things for me. Not only are you good at them, but the better and better you become at doing them for me, the more and more irreplaceable you make yourself. For me."

Jason continued her thought, "And since I'm helping you do things that are invaluable for the company, that makes me invaluable up the line as well."

"Right. Of course, if you just delegated a bunch of LVAs—"

"Less Valuable Activities?"

"Right! Clever, huh? Anyway," Tracy continued, "if you just delegated a bunch of LVAs to Candice and didn't fill up the extra time you just gained with MVAs, then I would definitely not be happy."

"And I definitely would not become invaluable," Jason added.

"You got it." Tracy turned to her computer screen. "I've got a conference call coming up here, but let's schedule some time to get together so I can start giving you a few of my LVAs."

CEO

For the first two weeks after their meeting, Jason felt a real difference in working with Tracy. She started delegating more responsibility and treating him less like a drone and more like someone who had something to contribute. They worked out a simple system to assist Jason with handling Tracy's scheduling. Tracy even asked Jason to begin to respond to some of her e-mail, which said a lot to Jason. Trust was gradually growing between them. The biggest shock to Jason was that she was actually making a consistent effort to *listen* to him, something he had rarely experienced even from his first days of working at GreenGarb as an intern.

Jason also began delegating some of his LVAs, Less Valuable Activities, to Candice—things like running errands and doing market research. This gave him a little more freedom to focus on some of his MVAs, such as improving sales copy and working on ad design.

However, the progress was short-lived. The typical emergencies started to occur. One of the Web sites they had planned to collaborate on for an extended campaign folded; a printer botched a major job; the sales team was putting pressure on marketing to make changes to their strategy. And these were just the beginning of the list.

Tracy returned to her default setting, which was managing in crisis mode. She gradually took back control of her calendar and communicated less and less with Jason. He did the same, as he found himself so wrapped up in dealing with Tracy's rapid-fire demands that he did not even have enough time to delegate work to the intern.

Tracy was issuing a set of orders one Monday morning as she and Jason walked down the hall together.

"Do you have all that?" Tracy asked as she pulled up an incoming message on her cell phone.

"Sure," said Jason. Then he stopped in thought as Tracy continued to walk down the hall without him. She got about six paces down the hall, realized Jason wasn't there, and turned around.

"Where did you go? I need you to keep walking with me. I've got a lot of stuff waiting for me at my office I've got to get working on immediately." Jason rubbed his head in thought, which aggravated Tracy even more. Sometimes he liked to think on things a little longer than Tracy was comfortable with—which today was about two seconds. "Jason?" she said, exasperated.

"What happened to our regular meetings?" he asked. "I felt like we were making good progress a couple of weeks ago. Now we're back to business as usual."

"Look, Jason." Tracy pulled her eyes away from her phone reluctantly. "I appreciate your effort to make yourself more valuable here and all that. I get it. We'll start working on it again once things calm down. But sometimes work just has to be done. What the company needs is more important than what you need. You need to be more of a team player and not think about yourself so much."

"But if we keep running around putting out fires like this, are we really working on our Most Valuable Activities?"

"Jason, I really don't have time for this. I—"

"Would you two come with me for a moment?" another voice said.

Jason and Tracy turned around quickly to see where the voice had come from. It was Helen, the CEO, who had apparently wandered by and overheard their conversation. She didn't wait for their reply—just turned around and gestured over her shoulder for them to follow.

They glanced briefly at each other, then quickly followed Helen down the long hallway back to her office. The walk seemed a bit longer than normal for Jason, who had never really had the chance to talk personally to the CEO before. *Here's my first opportunity, and I'm about to be reprimanded!* For what, he wasn't quite sure.

She opened the door and gestured to the small conference table in her office. "Please, have a seat." She held the door open for them as they dutifully took their chairs. "No need to look like children caught stealing from the cookie jar," Helen said as she closed the door. "You're not in trouble. I want to share something with you." She opened up the drawer of her perfectly organized desk, flipped through a couple of files, and pulled out a few pieces of paper. She handed copies to Jason and Tracy, who both looked puzzled. (See pages 58–59.)

"What is this?" Tracy asked.

"This is called a Work Time Budgeter," Helen replied. "It's a little something I learned from a friend not too long ago. I heard the conversation you two were having and thought this might help. It sounds like the two of you are getting caught up in the rush of the day. A little too much to do. Am I right, Jason?"

Jason tried to cover his surprise both that Helen knew his name and that she was asking him a question. "Um . . . yes. Well, no. I mean . . . we're just doing what we're supposed to be doing. Our jobs. So, no complaints." He forced a smile.

Helen said, "Oh, I know you're not complaining, Jason. Both you and Tracy always work hard and I really appreciate that. But I think perhaps the both of you work a little too hard, sometimes."

(From page 57)

CURRENT HOURS			STATED VALUE/HOUR			ACTUAL VALUE/HOUR

RANK	ACTIVITY		BOUNDARY			
	Travel		"Engaged" travel to, from, and during work (usually by car)			
	Wasting Time		Non-recreation such as addictions, mindless Web surfing, and so on			
I	Processing		Taking items from gathering points and deciding What, When, and Where			

Note: For a copy of this exercise and step-by-step instructions, see the Appendix.

Sal/Hr							
$/HOUR	CURRENT	HR	VISION	HR	TARGET	HR	☑
$0	~ 50% of total travel						
$0							
~ Value of highest	~ 28% of total						

BUDGET

"What?" Now it was Tracy's turn to look shocked. "But don't you want us—"

"Understand, Tracy. I'm not saying you shouldn't work hard. I'm just saying you work *too* hard. You're putting in too much effort for not enough result. I used to, as well. At least until I went through this exercise." She held up the chart. "First question: how many hours do you work in a week? I know you're both on salary, so you probably don't keep close track of the hours. Just give it your best guess, based on an average week in the last month. But make sure to include it all. That means include the travel time to and from work and time spent thinking about work when at home."

Tracy stifled a laugh. "Well, I had a number in my head until you said that last part. I'm always thinking about work . . . even when at home. So do I put twenty-four hours a day?"

"I know the feeling." Helen grinned. "But you sleep, don't you? You eat, as well. Occasionally you take a break from work—even mentally. But remember what we learned from Phil a few months ago about multitasking. You're really doing one thing or the other; you can't do two things at the same time. So count all the hours in which work 'wins,' even if it's winning only in your head."

Jason thought about the last month and tried to consider how much time he spent responding to e-mail and occasionally thinking about work. He put down seventy hours in the first box. He stole a quick glance at Tracy's paper and saw she had written eighty-five hours. She appeared stoically proud of the number.

"Now," Helen continued, "I'm going to ask you a tough question. You're not used to thinking about it this way because you've been paid on salary so long. How much would you say you are worth per hour? That goes in the 'Stated Value Per Hour' box."

"How would we figure that out?" Jason asked.

"I had the same question," Helen replied. "I was told to put down what I would charge someone to consult with them for an hour to teach them how to do what I do. I suppose you could do the same, or you could just put down what you'd be willing to work for per hour if someone else were to hire you."

Jason looked up in the air to think about his answer while Tracy scribbled something on her paper. He shrugged and wrote down $20. "Is this right?" he asked Helen.

Helen didn't look at his paper as she said, "What really matters is what *you* think, not me. This is the value you are giving yourself right now. Whether or not you're actually making that is a different question."

Jason thought about that for a moment and decided he must be worth more than $20 per hour, so he scratched it out and put $25 instead. Jason tried to glance casually at Tracy's paper but found she had covered up her answer.

"Now," Helen said solemnly, "here is the number that *really* matters. What is your *actual* value per hour? This isn't what you think you should be paid, but what you're actually making per hour that you

63

work. The math is simple. Just take your annual salary, divide by fifty-two for the number of weeks in a year, and then divide by the number of hours you're working each week."

Jason did the math, taking his annual salary, dividing by fifty-two, and then dividing by the seventy hours per week he estimated he was working. He was shocked as he wrote $9.61 in the "Actual Value/Hour" box.

He looked over at Tracy and saw even more disbelief on her face. She shook her head and grabbed Jason's paper to look at his answer. He ignored the impropriety of it, as he figured she knew what he was making already.

"What! I'm making less per hour than you are!" Tracy exclaimed. "That can't be right. Either you need to start working more, Jason, or I need a raise!"

"I'm getting a pretty good deal, huh?" Helen said mischievously. "I wish that were true, but it really isn't. I'm not getting a good deal . . . in fact, we're all getting a poor deal. You're working more hours than you should be working, but the company doesn't get any increase in productivity from it."

"What do you mean?" Jason asked.

"I mean your actual value per hour and your productivity are connected. Some people pride themselves on how many hours they work, not realizing what they are really doing is spending time in activities that are just wasting money *and* time. I can say that because I used to be one of them. I used to wear the hours I worked as a badge of honor. Now I realize it isn't about how many hours I work; it's what I really, truly accomplish during those hours that matters." She looked at Tracy and said, "Don't be too discouraged. When I did this exercise my actual value per hour was less than a third of what I thought I was worth."

Still a bit stunned, Tracy said, "So what do we do with the rest of this chart?"

"List all the different activities you perform at work. Some of them are more valuable than others, but go ahead and list them all. One way that's helpful to do this is to think of each activity as a mini-position, like trainer, writer, sales rep, or custodian." Jason and Tracy looked at each other. "What?" Helen asked, noticing the exchange.

"We just did something like this a few weeks ago," Tracy replied. "Well, not exactly like this, but we did start to list out all our activities to figure out which were our strengths and which were harder to replace than others."

"Good!" Helen said. "Then this first part should be simple for you. The 'Boundary' column to the right is to make sure you don't double count any work activity. For instance, if there is any possible overlap between being a 'manager' and a 'trainer,' you want to explain the difference so there's no possibility of double-counting your time."

"What are the 'Travel,' 'Wasting Time,' and 'Processing' rows for?" Jason asked.

"Those are three things everyone shares in common, to some degree, at work. Travel time is time traveling to, from, and for work. Wasting time is just that—wasting time. We all do it to some degree. And processing is a bit more complex, but for simplicity just think of it for now as checking your mail, e-mail, and voicemail. I'll explain more about processing in a bit."

"Got it."

Jason started by filling in the activities he had listed when he and Tracy had their meeting a few weeks ago. Then he added a little more description to the "Boundary" column to make sure there was a separation of the activities in his mind.

When he was done, Jason showed his worksheet to Helen. "How does this look?" (See pages 68–69.)

"Good!" said Helen. "How's yours coming, Tracy?"

Tracy was writing in the bottom margins of her paper in what looked like a scribbled mess. "This sheet isn't big enough for me. I have so many different jobs I do here!"

"I'm sorry." Helen shook her head and handed Tracy another blank worksheet. "I should have thought of that. You can just put your extra activities on another sheet. I had the same problem when I did this exercise. It's part of the challenge of being in a growing company like ours. People end up having many different jobs they need to juggle. Part of what we're going to accomplish with this work-sheet is help cut down on how many different jobs you perform—in a responsible way, of course."

Helen and Jason waited patiently for Tracy to finish. When she was done, Helen said, "Great. Now, skip over the '$/Hour' column for a moment. We'll come back to that shortly. Start by recopying the 'Current Hours' number at the top for the 'Current' column. So, Jason, you put seventy hours there—and, Tracy, you put eighty-five hours

(From page 67)

CURRENT HOURS	70	STATED VALUE/HOUR	$25 ~~$20~~	ACTUAL VALUE/HOUR
ACTIVITY			BOUNDARY	
Travel			"Engaged" travel to, from, and during work (usually by car)	
Wasting Time			Non-recreation such as addictions, mindless Web surfing, and so on	
Processing			Taking items from gathering points and deciding What, When, and Where	
Market research — Internet			Search internet for competitor and market data; gather for reports	
Writing Reports			Assemble reports for Tracy in a final presentation format	
Coordinate Focus Groups			Contact customers and invite them to participate; set up date, time, location	
Run Errands			Run to office supply store, etc.	
Calendaring for Tracy			Setting up appointments for Tracy with strategic partners	
Fielding Calls from Vendors			Act as gatekeeper	
Designing Materials			Improve or make new marketing designs for ads, websites, etc.	
Copywriting			Improve or write new company marketing copy	

Budget

$9.61			DATE	
$/HOUR	**CURRENT**	**HR**	**VISION**	**HR**
$0		~ 50% of total travel		
$0				
~ Value of highest		~ 25% of total		

there. Good. Now you need to estimate how much time you're spending in each of the activities you listed, starting with the three that were filled out for you: Travel, Wasting Time, and Processing."

"Why does it say 'fifty percent of total travel' in the Travel box?" Tracy asked.

"Good question," Helen replied. "That is because sometimes while you are traveling you can do other things, but sometimes you can't. For instance, while I'm sitting on the plane I can read through marketing reports you give me."

"But when you're going through airport security, you can't do anything else," Jason added.

"You've got it. The same can be said to some degree or another about driving. So, a safe guess for that row is to take all the time you are traveling and divide it in half."

They did so, and Helen continued. "Now, as I mentioned, 'Wasting Time' is pure wasted time. Of course, don't feel like you guys can't have a little fun occasionally."

Jason snickered to himself as he remembered one Halloween company party where Helen showed up dressed as a large toilet plunger. When he realized both women were looking at him, he said, "Sorry. Go ahead."

Helen smiled. "We have a fun culture at GreenGarb that I take pride in, but there's a difference between a small joke or even sharing a quick funny video on the Internet and spending hours surfing the Web."

Jason was a bit embarrassed to write down this number in front of the CEO. Tracy looked a little uncomfortable, too. Helen saw their discomfort and said, "Look, I'll make no judgment here. In fact, I don't even want to know what your number is. I just want *you* to know what the number is so you can decide what changes you want to make, without me looking over your shoulder."

Jason thought about the last few weeks. He wasn't a big fan of surfing the Internet, but he had spent a few hours each week discussing the latest sports events and TV shows with a few of his buddies at GreenGarb. Probably just a bit more than he should, but not too much. He guessed it was about thirty minutes a day, so he put down "2.5."

Helen was making a show of looking up at the ceiling while they wrote the numbers down. She looked at Tracy and Jason out of the corner of her eye.

"Done? Good. Now, processing is something special. I told you before that it represents you checking your mail, e-mail, and so on."

"Right, but it says 'Taking items from gathering points and deciding What, When, and Where' in the 'Boundary' column," Tracy said.*

"True. Processing is really just the act of deciding *what* you're going to do next with something, *when* you're going to do it, and *where* the thing belongs."

Tracy sighed. "Well, then, processing is pretty much my whole day. I'm always deciding What, When, Where. It never stops!"

"And that is part of the problem," Helen said as she pointed to Tracy. "It's why this box is grayed out in the 'Current' column. Because unless you establish a set time and a set place to do those things, your whole day will get chewed up processing. According to my consultant, Phil, the average person spends about 25 percent of their day processing when they don't have a schedule."

---

*For a simple What, When, Where processing chart, please see the Appendix.

Jason leaned back in his chair, stunned. "That's over seventeen hours a week for me! Wow."

"Seventeen?" Tracy scoffed. "For me it's almost twenty-one hours a week! That's a whole lot of time processing. But I have to do that, Helen, right? I mean, you need me to stay on top of things in order to keep the company running smoothly for you."

"True," Helen said quietly. "But my guess is you could probably get your processing done in six hours every week. Maybe even five."

Tracy stared in disbelief. "How is that possible?"

Helen smiled. "You certainly remind me of myself a few months ago, Tracy. It's all about the budget."

"The budget?" Jason asked. "What do you mean?"

"All I can tell you is that I probably used to spend about twenty-five hours a week processing before this exercise. Phil told me to schedule a set time and a set place every week for my processing and I should be able to get it done in five hours a week. I've found it actually takes me closer to seven hours. However, the principle is true: when I stick to my processing budget, I'm able to stay on top of everything. I gather everything in just a few places, and then have a set time every week to go through everything in those gathering points. By doing this instead of checking my e-mail and other stuff furiously throughout the day I can actually decide What, When, and Where for everything in just a short time."

Jason was starting to see the puzzle take shape in his mind. He hadn't quite assembled it yet, but he was beginning to see how what Charlie had said, what he and Tracy had talked about, and what Helen was now teaching them could fit together . . . somehow. "That's where we're headed with this whole exercise, right? You want us to not just budget our processing, but everything else, too."

Helen held up her hand. "Almost, we'll get there in a second." She pointed back to Jason's worksheet. "For now, just leave processing for 'Current' blank, but go ahead and put a '5' in the 'Vision' column." She turned to Tracy. "You put a '6' there, Tracy, because I think you'll need a bit more time.

"This means we're going to assume that, right now, processing is a part of everything else you've listed as an activity, but in the future you're going to budget the time and set it aside from everything else."

Jason and Tracy wrote that down, and Helen continued. "Now, estimate how much time you're currently spending in each of the activities. Don't worry about getting it to total up to the number of hours you said you were working—yet. And remember, this is based on an average week in the last month. Don't try to get it perfect. Just put your best guess for now and then we'll balance it out in the end."

Jason began writing down how much time he thought he was spending in marketing research each week. Then he continued with the "Writing Reports" row until he had filled out the entire chart. Tracy took a bit longer as she had more job activities.

When they were both done, Helen said, "Good. Now, try to make it balance up with the number of hours you estimated at the beginning."

"I'm five hours over budget," Jason said.

"Not bad. The first time I did an exercise like this I was about twenty-two hours off, if I remember right!" She laughed. "So you just need to figure out where you are over budget. Usually look for the areas where you are spending the most time. It is possible that you underestimated how many hours you're really spending working, as well."

Jason saw the calculator on Helen's desk. "Uh, may I?"

"Go right ahead," Helen said.

"I guess it's a good thing you didn't hire me for my math skills, huh?" Jason said sheepishly as he grabbed the calculator. He started to crunch the numbers. He realized that over the last month he was probably spending a few less hours doing Internet research than he originally thought, likely because he had already delegated some of that to Candice. He also raised his estimate of how many hours he thought he was working to seventy-two. When he was done, he showed his worksheet to Helen. (See pages 78–79.)

Tracy passed hers over the table, as well. Helen looked the budgets over carefully for a moment, then handed the papers back to them. "Fantastic! So, now that we have your current estimated budget in place, let's go back to the '$/Hour' column. This is where we put the 'Replacement Value Per Hour.'"

"What is the Replacement Value?" Tracy asked.

"It's what *you* would need to pay someone else to do that job for you. Specifically—give me a moment . . . " Helen shuffled through her previously marked-up pages. "Here it is. It's a pretty long definition: 'The amount of money per hour you would need to pay someone else to do this same job at the same level of effectiveness at which you currently perform.'"

"That's a mouthful," Jason said.

"Yes, it is, isn't it?" Helen nodded. "Basically, the key is, imagine *yourself* as the employer now, and you're going to hire someone else to replace you in that activity. What would you need to pay them?"

"As little as possible!" Tracy moaned. "I can't afford to give up any part of my paycheck to someone else."

"Ah, but that's the trick, Tracy. You can't pay just anyone just any amount. You have to pay someone who is *as effective as you are* in that activity without any further training. Understand, I'm not necessarily saying you're going to go out and hire someone to do the work for you. What we're doing is equating a value per hour to each activity, which will give us an idea of what activities are worth the most to the company."

Both Jason and Tracy laughed and said, almost in unison, "Your MVAs!"

"What's this?" Helen asked. "You two have some sort of inside joke?"

"Not a joke. Just a term I—"

(From page 76)

CURRENT HOURS	70	STATED VALUE/HOUR	$25 $20		ACTUAL VALUE/HOUR
ACTIVITY			BOUNDARY		
Travel			"Engaged" travel to, from, and during work (usually by car)		
Wasting Time			Non-recreation such as addictions, mindless Web surfing, and so on		
Processing			Taking items from gathering points and deciding What, When, and Where		
Market research — Internet			Search internet for competitor and market data; gather for reports		
Writing Reports			Assemble reports for Tracy in a final presentation format		
Coordinate Focus Groups			Contact customers and invite them to participate; set up date, time, location		
Run Errands			Run to office supply store, etc.		
Calendaring for Tracy			Setting up appointments for Tracy with strategic partners		
Fielding Calls from Vendors			Act as gatekeeper		
Designing Materials			Improve or make new marketing designs for ads, websites, etc.		
Copywriting			Improve or write new company marketing copy		

$9.61			DATE	
$/HOUR	CURRENT	7̶0̶ 72 HR	VISION	HR
$0	1.5 ~50% of total travel			
$0	2.5			
~Value of highest	~ 25% of total		5	
	1̶5̶ 12			
	15			
	5			
	15			
	5			
	4			
	6			
	5			

79

"We," Jason corrected.

"*We* came up with," Tracy continued. "We decided activities we were strong at doing and which would be difficult to find someone else to do were our Most Valuable Activities."

"MVAs for short," Jason added quickly.

"I see." Helen smiled. "I'm glad to see you two have been working together on something like this. So, let's find out if your assumptions about your . . . *MVAs* were correct, shall we?"

Jason and Tracy began creating arbitrary value per hour numbers for the activities listed on their chart. Helen explained that, for simplicity, they should just assume the person doing each activity would have a full-time job, so they could estimate an annual salary and divide by fifty-two for the weeks in the year and forty for the hours worked—or just divide by 2080.

Jason completed his chart and handed it to Helen. (See pages 82–83.)

"Good," said Helen. "Now, answer a question for me—there's no right or wrong answer. And please be candid. Compare the 'Replacement Value Per Hour' column and the 'Current' column. Look at how much time you're spending in your Most Valuable

Activities, and on the ones worth the least. Does anything stand out to you?"

Tracy laughed bitterly. "Oh yes. Something stands out to me for sure. I've been spending hours and hours doing online social media marketing when that is one of my lowest-value activities! I mean, it's important, but there are others who could do it just as well as me—if not better. I could be spending more time on much more valuable activities if I delegated that task. And that's just a start."

Jason looked at his list and saw a similar pattern. Design and copywriting were his two MVAs, yet he was spending more time running errands and writing reports, which were less valuable. "Well, and what I see, too," he said, continuing his thought out loud, "is there are activities on this list that I'm spending more time doing than necessary. Even if I still ran all the errands myself, I could be a whole lot more efficient if I grouped them together. I'm running them all over the place because I just do them whenever, rather than planning ahead. It's taking me fifteen hours a week right now because . . . well . . . I guess it's because I wasn't aware of how much opportunity I was wasting before looking at it this way."

(From page 80)

CURRENT HOURS	70	STATED VALUE/HOUR	$25 ~~$20~~	ACTUAL VALUE/HOUR
ACTIVITY			BOUNDARY	
Travel			"Engaged" travel to, from, and during work (usually by car)	
Wasting Time			Non-recreation such as addictions, mindless Web surfing, and so on	
Processing			Taking items from gathering points and deciding What, When, and Where	
Market research — Internet			Search internet for competitor and market data; gather for reports	
Writing Reports			Assemble reports for Tracy in a final presentation format	
Coordinate Focus Groups			Contact customers and invite them to participate; set up date, time, location	
Run Errands			Run to office supply store, etc.	
Calendaring for Tracy			Setting up appointments for Tracy with strategic partners	
Fielding Calls from Vendors			Act as gatekeeper	
Designing Materials			Improve or make new marketing designs for ads, websites, etc.	
Copywriting			Improve or write new company marketing copy	

Budget

$9.61			DATE	
$/HOUR	CURRENT	~~70~~ 72 HR	VISION	HR
$0	1.5 ~ 50% of total travel			
$0	2.5			
? ~Value of highest	/////// ~ 25% of total		5	
$10/hr	~~15~~ 12			
$12/hr	15			
$14/hr	5			
$8/hr	15			
$15/hr	5			
$9/hr	4			
$29/hr	6			
$24/hr	5			

Helen applauded them both briefly. "And that leads us right to the last column, the 'Vision' column. Up at the top put the date six months from now. Imagine your schedule once you have an opportunity to be strategic about your time budget. If you feel it's realistic, change the total hours you feel you will need to work to accomplish everything.

"Once you have that number, create a new budget for each activity on this list. Try to increase the time spent in MVAs and decrease the time you spend in the less valuable activities."

"We prefer to call them *LVAs*," Tracy said in mock ceremony.

"LVAs. Of course!" Helen laughed. "What you are ultimately doing is raising your actual value per hour. Remember the number we came up with at the top? That will begin to improve because you'll reduce the overall hours you're working, and you'll also be increasing your value as an employee because you'll be working in higher-value activities." She quickly added, "Of course, while still getting all the work done that is expected of you."

"But wait, uh, Helen," Jason said, unsure if he was on a first-name basis with his CEO yet. "I didn't put anything for processing. It says 'equal to value of the highest.' What does that mean?"

"Great question, Jason. I asked the same thing myself. It means that whatever is the highest-value activity you perform, you put that in the 'Replacement Value Per Hour' box for 'processing.'"

"Okay," Jason said as he wrote "$29/hr" in the box.

"But . . . why?" Tracy asked. "You said before we were being unproductive by jumping back and forth all day long making decisions about What, When, Where. Now you're telling us it's worth more than everything else?"

"Not worth *more,* just *equal to* the value of the highest," Helen explained. "When you properly engage in What, When, Where processing, you leverage your ability to stay focused in your . . . Most Valuable Activities. Your MVAs. Because when you don't process properly, when you're doing it all over the place, your day gets chewed up."

Tracy nodded slowly. "And you just end up jumping all over the place doing a little bit of every activity."

"Right," Helen said. "Of course, there are limits to that, as well. Let me draw a little graph I came up with to make it clearer in my mind." She flipped over a piece of paper and drew a simple bell curve on the back.

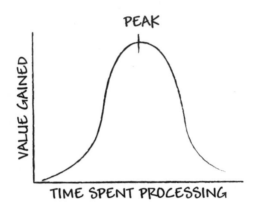

"I call it the 'Curve of Peak Processing Returns.' Sounds impressive, right? I'm an economics nerd now!" She laughed at herself shaking her head. Tracy and Jason glanced at each other briefly as Helen continued. "Basically, it says there is a 'sweet spot' for processing. Again, that's usually around five hours per week. The trick is to find what the peak amount of processing time is for your position right now and stick to it. No more, no less. It took me a bit of time to figure out seven was my magic number. But once I figured it out I really found my ability greatly improved in all areas.

"It also gave me the ability to start to protect the time I had set aside for *my* MVAs. Without regular, scheduled processing I would just do whatever, whenever. Now I decide clearly when I'm going to work on certain projects, and I budget them cleanly into my calendar for the amount of time per week I predetermined."

Jason pondered this for a bit. He realized there were many days where he was just jumping from task to task not even sure what he was working on at any given time. There were other days, however, when he seemed to sit and check e-mail mindlessly for hours. There was no clear pattern to how he used his time. He was just drifting like a small raft in the open sea. He had not taken control of his day. He definitely had not thought at all about whether he was spending enough time in his Most Valuable Activities. *I've been getting mad for feeling like a grunt, feeling like people were just heaping tasks on me and making me jump all over the place,* he thought. *But I've been doing it to myself!*

Quietly, he said, "'When you focus on your Most Valuable Activities, both your ability and the difficulty of replacing you are increased.'" Jason turned to Tracy. "That's what Charlie told me."

"Who said that?" Helen asked.

"Just a very wise old man," Jason smiled.

ENTREPRENEUR

Thwap!

Jason looked approvingly into the distance as his golf ball flew across the driving range.

"Nice one," his friend Samantha—Sam, he called her—said as she placed her own ball on the tee. "I can see you're getting almost as good as me. I'll have to practice more."

"*Almost* as good as you, huh?" Jason laughed as Sam drove a straight shot down the range. Meeting at the driving range had become a bit of a Saturday morning tradition for the two over the last couple of years. They had known each other since they were in grade school, and their paths had run parallel to each other ever since—with one exception. While Jason had opted for the corporate world, Sam had always had an entrepreneurial streak. They had graduated together from the same college, though Sam's GPA wasn't anywhere near Jason's. That wasn't because Sam wasn't as smart or as hard-working as Jason; the opposite was true. She had been so involved in her small but growing business—a chain of mall stands she had started their sophomore year—that college and grades had taken a backseat.

Sam shielded her eyes, looking for the ball. "That's easily another twenty yards past yours. What can I say?" She turned and grinned.

"There was a bit of a breeze just a moment ago. Watch this," he said as he took a hard swing. Sam attempted to contain a laugh as the ball sliced sharply off the driving range.

"So tell me about work," Sam said over her shoulder as she teed up her next shot. "How's life working for 'the man'?"

"Well, actually it's 'the woman.' But yeah, it's good. Things are starting to get a lot better. I'm starting to figure out how to become invaluable to the company."

"*Invaluable?* What does that mean?" Sam said, stopping her swing.

"Oh, basically it's about how to make myself harder for the company to replace. I'm learning to focus on the activities I do for GreenGarb that I'm good at and are worth the most per hour." Jason teed up another ball. "I'm working to increase my pay based on demand for what I do, my ability to do it, and the difficulty of finding somebody else to take it over. That's the short version of it, anyway." Jason took a swing while Sam stood in thought.

"So, what does your boss think about this? Isn't she worried that you're positioning for a raise? It seems to me you should be worrying more about how to make the company invaluable, not yourself."

"Actually, our CEO helped both me and my boss figure it out."

"I've *got* to meet Helen someday," Sam said. She had told Jason several times how much she admired what Helen had accomplished as an entrepreneur.

"She's started training other managers in some of the concepts for them to pass it along to their employees." He took his ball cap off to scratch his head for a moment. "We haven't really talked about making the company invaluable, though."

"Sure you have," Sam said. "Doesn't Helen have a vision or mission for the company? What about a unique selling proposition?"

Jason shrugged. "Sure. It's something like, 'clothing the world in an environmentally safe but profitable way.' I've heard it a bunch of times, so you'd think I'd have it memorized by now."

Sam now reached into her golf bag, pulled out her phone, and began typing a note to herself. If Jason hadn't known Sam as well as he did, he'd have thought she was ignoring him. *She never really turns that entrepreneurial brain off,* Jason thought, amused. Sam was constantly looking for ways to improve her business—she had been for as long as Jason knew her, even as a young girl. At times, it was a bit exhausting to be around, but she was his friend, so he put up with it. "Okay, boss. What did you type?" he asked.

"'How are we invaluable to our customers?'" Sam quoted from her notepad. "I think that's a question I really should be asking about Fresh 'N Juicy as a whole. You mentioned something before . . . what were the three things that determined how valuable you are?"

"Demand. Ability. Irreplaceability. But really, you have little control over demand, so you have to focus on your ability to do something and the difficulty of replacing you. When you focus on your Most Valuable Activities, both your ability to do whatever it is and the difficulty of replacing you are . . . increased . . ." Jason trailed off as he realized Sam was making more notes in her pad.

"What is our ability as a juice stand? How easy is it for our customers to replace us?" Sam thought out loud. *Here comes one of her entrepreneurial rants,* Jason thought. "I think it's easy to assume that customers will just show up because we have a great product. I mean, we work to make a great juice and I try to make it the way I'd like it, but I'm not considering the demand much. I definitely have not been thinking about how replaceable we are. I mean, I'm aware of our competition in the mall. But I've been viewing our competitors more as rivals for sales, rather than as a legitimate purchase option for the customer.

"Maybe I should be asking regularly what we are doing to make ourselves the 'juice of choice' for shoppers at the mall. What are we doing to make ourselves more valuable to our customers?"

"Better add another question to ask yourself: 'What can I do today to become more valuable?'" Jason said, teasing her. But he sighed and rolled his eyes as he saw Sam nodding solemnly and writing in her notepad again. Sam was a great friend but sometimes she got just a bit too intense about business for Jason's liking.

"That is a great idea, Jason," Sam said in all seriousness.

Jason shook his head, mumbling to himself as he put another ball on the tee. He started his swing just as Sam asked, "So, what did Helen tell you?" The ball sliced wildly again. Jason glared at Sam. "Sorry," she said quietly. "I meant about the invaluable thing. You mentioned she helped you. What did she say you should do?"

"Well, it's pretty simple, really. She said we needed to identify our Most Valuable Activities—we call them MVAs—"

"Clever."

"Always!" Jason grinned as he continued, "And we needed to budget more time to spend in them. She also said we needed to identify our Least Valuable Activities, or LVAs, and spend less time in them." Jason hesitated.

"What?"

"Well, I think that's where I may be having a problem. I seem to be spending way too much time in Least Valuable Activities. I'm stuck doing them and can't seem to get out."

Sam laughed. "You mean sort of like what happens to you out on the course? You always manage to find a way to end up in the sand traps and can't get out of them."

"Cute," Jason said. "Although that's probably pretty true. I keep getting caught in these . . . 'LVA traps' and have a hard time getting out of them. The little minutiae of the day grab me and pull me away from my MVAs. Even though I know I shouldn't check my e-mail all day long or I know I should delegate a task like running to the store, it just seems easier to do it myself. I want to spend more time in my MVAs than I am right now, but it seems like I can't afford to have someone else take care of the LVAs for me."

"I deal with that same problem every day." Sam paused for a moment and cleanly drove a ball across the range with a satisfying pop. She continued, "There never seems to be enough time for everything I need to do. I feel like I should hire more people, but at the moment, things are tight.

"It's a chicken-and-egg thing. How do you afford to hire the people you need when you don't have the people you need to make the money you need to hire the people?" Sam sighed. "If you find an answer, let me know."

"Well, we'll figure it out . . . somehow." Jason scowled as he took another swing, and his last range ball hooked off into the trees.

"Well, whatever you do, you may want to consider getting a coach for that swing. Your technique is a bit off," she teased.

Jason stopped. "What did you just say?"

"I said, you might want to get a golf coach, but I was just—"

"Sam, you're brilliant!" Jason said as he dropped his clubs quickly into his bag. As he walked off he said, "See you next Saturday!"

TRAPS

Tracy shook her head at Jason. "I can't believe you actually asked the CEO for permission to have her consultant come in and talk to us. We give you just a little bit of attention, and you think you're running the place!"

"First of all, he's a coach, not a consultant," Jason replied. "And second, all I'm doing is trying to make myself more valuable."

"And where does meeting with the business coach figure in to your copywriting and design work? I thought those were your two MVAs."

Jason shrugged. "Well, I guess you have me there. Maybe part of one of my MVAs is to become an expert in becoming invaluable? All I know is

Helen was excited about the idea, provided you and I both report back to her what we learned."

There was a knock at the door and a man poked his head in. "Am I in the right place?" Phil asked as he stepped in. "I think I've seen you around before. You're Tracy and you're Jason, the intern, right?"

"*Former* intern," Tracy said. "He was hired a few months ago and I think he's due to be promoted to VP here in a couple of days."

"I see," Phil said as he took a seat beside Tracy's desk. "Well, Helen said you two would like to meet with me. How can I help?"

Tracy pointed to Jason. "Ask him—this was his big idea."

"Thanks for coming, Phil," Jason said a bit nervously. "I have a question for you."

"Okay. I'll see what I can do to help. What is your question?"

Jason cleared his throat. "Well, basically we're trying to solve the chicken-and-egg problem."

"Okay . . ." Phil said slowly.

"What I mean," Jason continued, "is we're trying to figure out how to spend less time in our LVAs. Uh, did Helen talk to you about that? The MVA-LVA thing, I mean?"

"LVAs are Least Valuable Activities. MVAs are Most Valuable Activities. Yes, Helen has told me in our meetings what you two have been working on. I really like the idea. Go on."

"What I've found is that we're both getting caught up in LVA traps—at least I am," Jason said.

"LVA *traps?*" Phil raised his eyebrows. "Helen didn't mention those, I believe."

Tracy held her hands up in a shrug. "This is news to me too. What are you talking about, Jason?"

"Sorry, it's a little term a friend of mine came up with. LVA traps are anything that causes you to spend more time than you should in an LVA. Things like interruptions, random assignments from nowhere, getting caught up in minor details, and just not knowing how to delegate properly." Jason looked at them both carefully to make sure they were following along. *I'm probably making a fool of myself,* he thought. "I really want to make it work to spend more time in my MVAs, but I keep getting stuck in LVAs. They pull me in. Sometimes I feel they're just part of my job and there's nothing I can do about it. I was hoping you could help."

Phil nodded slowly and then reached into his briefcase. "I think I get where you are coming from."

He pulled out a piece of paper. "But let me be sure we're on the same page. Forgive me . . . I like to draw pictures to help me visualize things."

He drew a simple graph on the page.

"What I understand is this: your time at work is limited." Phil saw Tracy rolling her eyes and quickly added, "At least to some degree, right? Your LVAs and your MVAs are at odds with each other. The more time you spend in LVAs the less time you have to spend in MVAs. Right?"

"Right," said Jason.

"But LVAs have a lot of pull to them. They're easier. They're often more demanding, but really, they take less effort. It's just their nature. If it's easier to do, then more people are doing it, and therefore it's easier to replace yourself with someone else to do that task. That's what makes it an LVA."

Tracy was surprised. "I hadn't thought of it that way!"

Jason, however, said, "I'm not sure I understand."

"You're naturally going to be drawn toward doing LVAs, even if you're not as good at them. That's because they're simple and easy to replace. Which takes less effort, going to the store to pick up some pencils, or writing a marketing report or sales copy?" Phil asked.

"Obviously the errands," Jason replied.

"Right," Phil said, "and the same is true for surfing the Internet versus making phone calls to set appointments. LVAs require less energy to get going. They are easier for just about anyone to do, which makes it easy to replace you if you do them.

"That doesn't necessarily mean MVAs are less enjoyable. I'd certainly rather be training you two right now than running errands! But what it does say is that it takes more effort to get going in an MVA than an LVA. It takes more practice, more skill. More inertia.

"And that really is exactly what I need to change about this graph." Phil turned the graph on its side.

"Huh?" Now it was Tracy's turn to look confused.

"I get it," Jason said. "LVAs are like the gravity of the earth. They always pull you down, away from your MVAs."

"Right. And just like a hot air balloon, the more activities you have on board, the harder it is to get off the ground. It really doesn't matter how many are MVAs or LVAs. You can only really have a couple of Most Valuable Activities anyway. Every activity you perform, whether it's an LVA or an MVA, is a sand-bag for the balloon. Got it? So when you have more activities to perform—"

"It's harder to focus on your most valuable ones," Jason said.

"Right. This is why I've found most business owners spend most of their time in LVA—not MVAs. Of course, I didn't use those terms before, since you two came up with them," Phil said, smiling at them both. "But business owners, entrepreneurs, and many executives get sucked into lots of little things. Even more so than, say, a middle manager or a front-line employee—"

"Because they are carrying so many different activities in their balloons!" Tracy jumped in. "That's how I feel right now, even though I'm not really a business owner."

Phil nodded. "Well, part of that is because you're working in a small but growing business. In situations like this, everyone gets more bags on their balloon in comparison to the employee working at a large, established company. You're asked to do many different things."

"But that causes us to all get pulled toward the ground—toward our LVAs!" Jason exclaimed. "So that's the problem, Phil. How do we get out of it?"

"That's a great question, and I believe I have the answer." He flipped over the piece of paper. "We need to offload the sandbags."

OFFLOADING

"It sounds simple, Phil," Tracy said. "Just dump the sandbags. But where do we do that? I mean, it's not like we have the resources to go out and hire a bunch of people to do little things. Some of the things I do are only three- to four-hour-a-week jobs at best. How do I offload those?"

"I have a decision-making system I use with my clients," Phil said. "I call it 'The Order of Offloading.' It's basically a logical process for deciding the best way to offload and when to do it." Phil began writing a list on the paper:

1. *Personal systems*
2. *Business systems*
3. *Technology*

4. *Outsourcing*
5. *Hire*

"So, the first place to start is by improving your personal systems. These are things like how you handle e-mail, voicemail, interruptions, filing, and so on. Most people can find an extra ten to twenty-five hours per week just by improving their personal systems alone. That's the equivalent of an extra workweek every single month!"

"I remember Helen talking about that," Tracy said, "how multitasking is so counterproductive in the workplace."

"Right," Phil said. "Building personal systems usually helps you cut out a lot of switches in your day, which are so costly to your time. *Switching cost*—the transition time between tasks—alone is one huge LVA that is worth nothing per hour."

"Is that what Helen meant when she was talking about budgeting time for processing?" Jason asked.

"She taught you about processing?" Phil smiled. "Good! Yes. When you can make decisions about What, When, and Where at a regularly scheduled time, you will greatly protect your MVAs. In fact, I'd say processing is the foundation system for all other personal systems." He looked at each of them. "How have you been doing with your processing time? Have you been sticking to it in your schedule?"

"Pretty much," Jason said.

"I could do better," Tracy replied. "I find other things just get in my way so often."

"That's pretty normal, at least in the beginning," Phil reassured her. "Just be careful that your processing time is scheduled at times in the day when you are least likely to be interrupted. It has to be a special time, removed from everything else, where you can focus on each item one at a time. If you allow yourself to be distracted by the phone ringing or e-mail arriving, having a set processing time will lose its effectiveness."

He turned his attention back to the list. "Okay, number two, business systems."

"Are those like our procedures and checklists at GreenGarb?" Jason asked.

"Right." Phil nodded. "Very often, a business winds up having a great deal of excess labor capacity. Here's one common example: a company hires someone to fill a position for forty hours a week. However, the actual job only requires thirty hours, so the new employee soon finds ways to stretch and slow down work to fill the full time.

"With a lack of solid business systems, including a good organizational structure, it's very easy for employees to have their time filled up with LVAs."

"Well, not only that," Tracy added, "But they're just wasting time in general because they have to ask their boss over and over how to do something. I'm sure you're talking about documented systems, right? Some way the employee can refer back to the training and not have to remember all the instructions?"

Phil gave her a thumbs-up. "You've got it. How well documented are the systems at GreenGarb—not the whole company, but just here in the marketing department?"

Tracy sighed. "Ah. I was feeling good until you added that last part! I mean, I know the production systems are well documented, but here in marketing . . . it just hasn't seemed like a fit before. What we do is so creative, so loose. How can we document processes that seem to be different every time?"

"That's a great question, Tracy," Phil replied. "I'll grant you some functions in a business aren't easy to document. The problem, however, usually arises when people try to document too much. They try to cover too much detail in a single system, which stifles creativity in employees.

"A good business system should be brief, a single page at most. It should just be a quick reference point for jogging the memory, not a detailed set of step-by-step instructions for every possible outcome. I'll give you a simple template later that you can use to help you with this."[*]

"Thanks," Tracy said.

"For more advanced clients, I've even shown them how to set up a wiki—an internal database—just for systems within the company. Then the employees can review and edit each other's work, becoming collaborators in developing company systems." Phil stopped. "But I'm getting a bit ahead of things, aren't I?"

Jason was still uncomfortable. "Something about this doesn't seem right to me, Phil. I mean, I'm sure what you're saying is right, but I'm not seeing how it fits in with becoming invaluable. In fact, if I document the way I do something, won't that make me easier to replace?"

"I see," Phil said quietly. "So you're asking me if you become an expert in how to do something

---

[*]For the Single Page system template and instructions, see the Appendix.

by figuring out how to turn it into a system, then suddenly the company is going to have no more use for you?"

"Well, uh, yeah. I guess that is what I'm saying."

Phil smiled, reached into his briefcase, and pulled out a golf magazine. "Ever read one of these?"

Jason had to laugh. "I have, actually. Funny you should ask. I got the idea to have you talk to us while I was out hitting balls on the range with my friend Sam."

"Who's Sam?" Tracy asked. "You've never mentioned him before."

"Sam's a girl." Tracy raised an eyebrow as Jason continued. "Anyway, Sam mentioned I should get a golf coach to improve my swing, and I thought I should ask a business coach how to improve my ability to become invaluable."

"Smart friend," Phil said. "So, you know from reading these things that there is always something to improve, always some small aspect of the game you can learn. This is because even though you may *know* something intellectually, even though you may have read it hundreds of times, you still haven't changed your muscle memory. You'll default to old habits without an expert outside to keep reminding you of the fundamentals."

"That's what you do as a business coach, right?" Jason asked.

Phil smiled knowingly. "And that's what you'll do as a systems expert."

"Systems expert?" Tracy asked. "What do you mean?"

"As the person who knows the system inside and out, you become even more valuable. You become someone the company needs . . . even more valuable and difficult to replace than before. When you become a systems expert through documenting a system in your business, suddenly you are an authority. You are someone who can teach—or coach—others in the company."

"Or manage," Tracy said absently. "That's what I should be doing more of."

"Absolutely!" Phil pointed to Tracy. "While both are necessary to a company, who is ultimately more valuable . . . someone who can make a widget, or someone who can train a hundred other people to make widgets?" Both Jason and Tracy nodded, knowing the answer to the question. Phil continued.

"So, if you want to free up your time *and* make yourself invaluable in the process, begin documenting the systems for your position and start teaching them to someone else."

"Wow, that sounds like I'll have less time," Jason thought out loud.

"Budget," Tracy said quickly. "It's all about the budget." She made a note for herself and then asked Phil, "What about technology?"

"That's a fun one," Phil said. "New, amazing technology tools are developed every day. This is why I subscribe to the best technology magazines. I want to be an invaluable resource for my clients in helping them make the best choices available. Simple technology improvements can be valuable time assets, releasing precious minutes and hours back into your workweek.

"For instance, if you are using a five-year-old computer that slows your productivity down by just 2 percent, a simple upgrade can yield about an hour per week to your time budget. That's like getting an extra work week every year!"

Tracy looked around her office. "It seems pretty straightforward. So how do I identify when I should make a technology upgrade?"

"Well," Phil said, "I try to look for continuously repetitive tasks in my day; anything I do over and over again. Then I search for a technological shortcut for it."

Jason squinted in thought. "Can you give me an example?"

"Sure." Phil thought for a moment. "Well, this is a bit oversimplified, but imagine you have to type the phrase, 'GreenGarb is Invaluable' more than twenty times per day. That's a hundred times per workweek and fifty-two hundred times per year. It really starts to add up over time. So you get a simple bit of software that provides a shortcut for you. You just type Control+Shift+Space+I and it automatically types the phrase for you. It seems like a small thing, but can really free up some valuable time."

Tracy looked at her computer screen. "I guess that's why I have an automatic signature at the bottom of every e-mail, right? It would be pretty slow for me to type all those details of my signature, phone number, fax number, and so on, over and over."

Jason chimed in. "Or why I carry around a Smartphone with all my contacts and my calendar. It saves me from having to look up a business card all the time."

"Right," Phil said. "The list of ways to cut LVA time using technology is endless and constantly growing. It's just important to remember not to spend more time finding and implementing a technology change than you're actually going to save in the end.

"In fact, I'd propose a rule of thumb: if you're not going to make up the time and money you'd invest in a new technology within one month, and if the change won't benefit you for at least a year, it's probably not worth the trouble."

Tracy snorted and rolled her eyes. "You should tell that to IT. It seems like we're getting some new system every year that takes up more time than we gained."

Phil smiled. "Technology for the company certainly applies; however, I'm referring mostly to you making personal investments to improve your productivity. From what I understand about this whole Invaluable movement you guys started, it's about you taking control of your own destiny.

"While getting a company requisition is certainly the optimal way to go, there's nothing that says you can't invest some of your own money to improve your own market value."

Both Jason and Tracy were silent at that thought. The idea of spending his own personal money to improve how well he performed at work didn't sit well with Jason—at least not yet. "I suppose if I knew for certain that making an investment would result in a raise, then I would do it."

"Remember the 'Time Value' calculation Helen showed you, Jason?" Phil asked. "She showed you that, right?"

"Yes."

"So, what happens to your actual value per hour the more hours you work?"

Jason nodded slowly. "It goes down. I get it. If I work less hours and still get the same work done, then I *am* giving myself a raise, right?"

Phil just grinned slightly. "So many people focus entirely on what they make per year. While that's important from a budgetary standpoint, what matters most is what they are actually making per hour. How would you like to make $100,000 per year, Jason?"

"I'd say 'when do we start?'" He smiled widely.

"Me too," Tracy chimed in.

"But what if I tell you you'd have to work a hundred hours per week? Would you be willing to do that?"

Jason frowned and shook his head. "Honestly, no. Maybe for a few weeks I could do it, but that's very little money for the time." Jason paused for a moment in thought. "But what if I used the order of offloading and upgraded my technology? Maybe even outsourced some of my work? What if I figured out a way to work, say forty-five hours per week, but get one hundred hours per week worth of work done by investing $35,000 per year in tools and upgrades to my personal systems? That would leave me with $65,000, which would still be a nice raise from where I'm at now!"

"Now you've got the picture." Phil grinned. "By the way, the $100,000 position's not available."

"And I was about to print out my résumé!" Tracy said.

Phil chuckled and continued, "And that leads us to the last two steps in the order of offloading. Outsourcing and hiring.

"Is there an outsource solution that will work for the needs you have? Could you hire a print broker instead of doing it all yourself? Could a professional graphic designer do a better job on that large project you are working on? There are even little outsourcing options, such as online companies that will proofread documents for you or transcribe your dictation. When you consider outsourcing work to a company, make sure their company values match yours. Otherwise, they may end up embarrassing you in front of your customers!"

Tracy pointed menacingly to Jason and said, "Or your boss!"

Phil continued, "If you have gone through 'The Order of Offloading' and found each of these steps has not solved the problem, or if you see you have unfilled business needs that would add up to a part- or full-time position, then it may be time to make a new hire.

"I know a few sales executives who, from their own commissions, without company funding, hired an assistant to do things like set appointments and send thank-you cards. The result in the cases I've seen is they dramatically increased their capacity and doubled their income or more with no more hours worked.

"The key, even for you as an employee, is to make sure you have business systems in place for the individual you hire. This will allow them to make an immediate impact the moment they are hired.

Don't just bring someone on and expect them to be perfect."

"Well," Tracy offered, "and realize if you weren't mentoring employees before, you'll now need to. You'll be adding more employee management—not to mention their payroll—to your job description!"

"I couldn't have said it better, Tracy," Phil said. "And what you just said is a big reason why I put making the hire at the bottom of the list. Not only is it the most expensive option, but it ultimately ends up putting a sandbag back in your balloon. I'm not saying you can't successfully offload activities this way, but it takes more practice and careful planning than the other methods."

Jason felt worn out and had a bit of a headache. "That's a lot of information you just threw at us."

"Sort of like reading a golf magazine? It's one thing to learn technique; it's another to implement it." Phil grinned. "Tell you what. I'll talk to Helen and see if she would like me to meet with you both a few more times to help put some of these things into place. We'll fine-tune your personal systems and help you start writing some business systems."

"That would be great, Phil," Tracy said. "We really appreciate it."

"No problem." Phil started to close up his brief-case to go and then paused for a moment. He pulled out a small notepad and made a note to himself. "Come to think of it, I may even work up a little test so we can measure your progress toward becoming invaluable."

"How can we do *that?*" Jason asked.

"I have my ways. See you two soon."

FACTOR

"Thanks for coming, Helen," Tracy said as she pulled out a chair for her CEO next to Jason and Phil.

"I thought you might like to see something," Phil said.

Helen sat down as Jason proudly presented her with two binders full of documents. "What's this?"

"These are my position systems," Jason said proudly, tapping a binder. "Each page is a single system. It's not everything I do at GreenGarb, but it's at least all the things I do at least once a week."

Helen pulled out her reading glasses and slowly flipped through the pages. She stopped at the page titled *Conduct Market Research*. "Impressive. I like how you fit each system onto a single page. It gives me the gist of what you need to do with a quick glance." She pulled out the second binder. "What is this?"

"My position systems," Tracy said. "Over the last few months, we both have been documenting everything we do regularly in our positions. Phil gave us the template, and we just followed his directions."

"We've also put these up on the company wiki," Jason chimed in. "Uh, you know, a place where everyone in the company can share information online," he added as Tracy rolled her eyes.

Helen smiled slightly. "I'm not *that* old, you know. I know what a wiki is. Who do you think ordered ours set up?" Jason mumbled an apology as Helen continued, "I like this. But the real question is, are you *using* it? I've seen a lot of companies—including this one—spend time writing systems that never end up getting read or used."

Tracy looked at Phil as if she expected him to answer. When he didn't, she replied, "Well, we've been using our employee-manager huddles to go through them. I check Jason's work, give him a little feedback to improve them. Then we go through some training that goes into more detail than what's written there. It really doesn't take that long to review a system or two. We spend about fifteen minutes a week."

Jason added, "And I also review it every once in a while when I'm working—just when I need a refresher. I mean, I'm not following the system word for word and step by step every time, but it is a helpful reminder. Sort of a guideline. I think it's really helped me get better at my job. Tracy doesn't need to repeat things to me anymore."

"What he means is, I'm bugging him less!" Tracy laughed.

"I wasn't going to say it . . ." Jason said sheepishly.

Helen nodded her approval. After a moment more of review, she closed the binders and looked Jason in the eye. "But the real question is, 'Are you invaluable?' Isn't that what you set out to answer in the beginning, Jason?"

Jason replied in mock smugness, "Well, my invaluable Score is up twenty points from where it was three months ago. I was a ninety, but now I'm a one-ten."

Helen raised her eyebrows and looked to Phil. "Can you translate? What is he talking about?

Up twenty points? One-ten? We haven't given you a raise yet that I'm aware of!"

"Jason's talking about his Invaluable Score," Phil said.[*]

"Invaluable Score?" Helen laughed. "What's that?"

Phil smiled. "It's an assessment I created to help him quantify his market value and identify the factors that he can improve to make himself Invaluable. It's an indicator of his market value in relation to his position, just like an IQ test is an indicator of your relative intelligence. And no, it doesn't mean you need to give him a raise—"

"Yet!" Jason cut in quickly.

"Yet," Phil agreed. "It's more of a predictor of personal market value over time. It's still up to him to prove that he deserves a raise here at GreenGarb." Tracy cleared her throat, and Phil added, "Tracy, of course, is too humble to mention it, but she actually has increased thirty-five percent from when she first took the assessment."

"Thank you," Tracy said in satisfaction.

---

[*] You can get a free light version of your personal Invaluable Score at www.InvaluableScore.com.

"I'm still refining the system," Phil continued, "but basically a score of one-ten means he's somewhat above average in his market value, just like an IQ test. One hundred is average, below sixty is easily replaceable, and over one-forty is, well . . ."

"Invaluable," Helen finished his sentence. "You'll have to take me through that . . . Invaluable Score sometime, Phil."

"Absolutely."

Helen looked appraisingly at both Jason and Tracy. "You two certainly have been busy, haven't you? I'm glad Phil was able to help you out."

"It wasn't me. They're the ones who did the work," Phil said as Tracy and Jason tried their best to appear humble.

"Yes, I can see." Helen rose from the desk. "Well, I need to get back to *my* MVAs. Thank you for showing me this, Phil."

"My pleasure."

"Not bad," Helen said as she opened the door to leave. "Not bad at all."

REPORT

"You do and it'll be the biggest mistake you ever made, you Texas brush-popper!"

Jason slowly opened the door. "Charlie?" he said loudly over the sound blaring from the television.

"Jason," Charlie said, hurriedly turning the volume down. He looked up at the clock, which said 5:15 PM. "You're here early. It's good to see you. You want to watch *True Grit* with me? It's one of your favorites, right?"

"Maybe," Jason said. "But first, I wanted to give you a little bit of a report . . . you know, about how things have been going for me at work. I know it's been awhile since we had that discussion—it was months ago, and I wanted to update you."

"Oh, have you figured out how to make yourself invaluable yet?" Charlie asked with a grin. Then seriously, he said, "Or maybe I should ask whether or not you quit your job?"

Jason put on a very concerned look. "Well, actually, I don't have my old job anymore. It wasn't a fit for me."

Charlie raised his eyebrows, but spoke steadily. "All right, son, if that's what you feel you needed to do, then . . . obviously it was the right choice, so I'll support you in it."

"Yes, well, I had been spending so much time with Tracy trying to figure out how to become more valuable in my position, I guess they didn't really want me in that position anymore," he sighed and paused. "So they gave me a promotion."

Charlie shook his head and mumbled, with a smile, "You need to not tease your grandpa so much. I get more trusting in my old age, you know."

There was a knock at the door. "Am I in the right place?"

Charlie peered around Jason's shoulder. "You've brought me a guest? Who is this young lady with you?" He started to stand up from his couch.

"Charlie, this is Tracy, my boss. Tracy, this is . . . well, you know who he is."

"Of course, I do." Tracy smiled. "I told Jason I wanted to leave work early today to come and give the man who helped me get a promotion a big hug." She gave Charlie—who was grinning ear to ear—a friendly hug.

Charlie then gestured for her to have a seat. "Promotion? But I thought Jason was the one who got the promotion."

"You told him already?" Tracy asked Jason. "Well, thanks to the advice you gave Jason, we *both* started working on becoming invaluable. The ideas you gave Jason really made a difference, not just for us but for the company, as well. I was able to implement changes in marketing I had been putting off for over a year. We saw a huge increase in sales."

"They made her VP of Sales and Marketing," Jason jumped in. "Helen—she's our CEO—said the growth was good enough that we needed to expand a bit."

Charlie looked thoughtful for a moment. "But you called her your boss, Jason. So if she was promoted, then . . ."

Tracy glanced at Jason, and replied, "When Helen promoted me, she asked who I thought would be best to take my old position. Your grandson was at the top of my list of recommendations."

Charlie applauded them. "Well done, well done, both of you!" To Jason he said, "I knew you had it in you, son. Just the first of more good news from you in the future, I'm sure."

Jason beamed. "Thank you, Charlie, but it was really you who started it all. You taught me about how to focus on my Most Valuable Activities. Others were helpful, too. But it was you who started it all."

"Nonsense!" Charlie sputtered. "You were the one who did the work. I just gave you a little nudge, that's all. I'm very, very proud of you, Jason." He rubbed his hands together. "Well, let's celebrate! I'll make up a bowl of my famous cheese popcorn and we can all watch the movie together. It's not that far in, I'll just start over. Do you like John Wayne, Tracy?"

Jason said quickly, "Uh, I don't know if Tracy was planning on staying that long, Charlie—"

Tracy waved him to be quiet. "No, it's okay, Jason. Honestly, Charlie, I'm not really much of a

Western movie fan," Tracy said. "But I have heard you're quite the chess player. I actually won a few tournaments when I was a girl."

Charlie raised his eyebrows. "Really! Well, then . . ." Charlie gestured to Jason, who reluctantly went to pull out the chessboard. "Now, don't expect me to go easy on you, just because you're Jason's boss." He winked.

"I wouldn't want it any other way, Charlie," she said. "It will make my victory even better knowing you gave it your all." She winked back.

Jason sighed and plopped onto the couch. "Well, while you two are having fun beating each other up on the chessboard, I guess I'll finish the movie."

He pushed a button on the remote and settled in to the familiar drawl of the Duke.

APPENDIX

ADVANCED STRENGTHS CHART

Result

This worksheet will help you quickly identify your personal MVAs, or Most Valuable Activities.

Steps

1. Using the worksheet on page 139, begin in the Work Activity column by listing all of the activities you performed in an average work-week in the last month. For a list of common work activities see the list on pages 137–138.
2. In the Strength # column, rate each activity as a 1, 2, or 4 in terms of whether it is a strength of yours. If you need help, speak to a supervisor or someone who is familiar with your work and will give you their candid opinion.

   1 = This is an activity others consider you *average or less than average* at doing.
   2 = This is an activity others consider you *above average* at doing.
   4 = You are recognized by others as an *industry leader* in this activity.

135

3. In the Replace # column, rate each activity from a scale of 1 to 10 in terms of how easy you feel it would be to find someone else in your job market who could do this activity well *and* is willing to do it. If you need help with this step, do a search online for the number of people doing this activity.

   1 = Any person could do this well and it would be easy to hire someone.
   3 = Most people can do this well and it would be relatively easy to hire someone.
   5 = Many people can do this well and someone could be hired with some effort.
   7 = Some people can do this well but the hiring process may be difficult.
   9 = Few people can do this well and the hiring process would be very difficult.
   10 = It would be nearly impossible to find someone else who can perform this activity well for any amount of money.

4. Multiply the Strength # by the Replace # column, and put the result in the Score column.
5. Compare your results to the following scale for a reality check. If your resulting score varies

from what the market is willing to pay you for that activity, then you may need to adjust your answers. (Typically, people underestimate how easy it is to find suitable replacements in an activity.)

1–4 = About minimum wage
5–9 = Entry-level wages
10–20 = Middle-class income
21–35 = Executive-level income
36–40 = Top income producers in the world

6. Finally, use the Rank column to rank each of the activities based upon the result in the Score column. Your top two or three results are your current MVAs. All other activities would be your LVAs, or Least Valuable Activities.

Common Work Activities

- Cleaning up
- Networking
- Employee management
- Visionary work
- Collections
- Research
- B2B sales
- Retail sales
- Web design
- Board meetings
- Financials
- Write systems

- Hiring and firing
- Training
- Writing
- Payroll
- Analyze financials
- Develop partnerships
- Legal
- Run errands
- Graphic design
- Customer service
- Route calls
- Build widgets
- Business development
- Mentor others
- Plan meetings
- Marketing
- Take product orders
- Many more . . .

Advanced Strengths Chart Worksheet

Work Activity	Strength # (1, 2, or 4)	Replace # (1–10)	Score	Rank

ADVANCED WORK TIME BUDGETER

Result

This worksheet will help you create a budget for improving the amount of time you spend in your Most Valuable Activities. It will help you identify which activities you should work on replacing first. Then it will help you create the beginning action steps for offloading those activities.

Steps

1. Using the worksheet on pages 148–149, begin by putting the number of hours you are currently working per week in the box next to Current Hours. For the purpose of this exercise, define working hours to include travel time to and from work, as well as time spent doing work or thinking about work at home.
2. In the box next to Stated Value/Hour, put what you would tell someone who asked you what you think you are worth per hour. Imagine you met someone at a conference who wanted to know how much you would charge to consult

about doing what you do. How much would you charge? Write that number in the box.

3. Now determine your actual value per hour and post it in the next box to the right. Your actual value per hour is your total annual take-home salary, including the value of any financial benefits or bonuses, divided by 52 (for weeks in the year), divided by your answer in the Current Hours box. This number is what you are *actually* making for every hour you work. For many, this number is significantly less than their stated value per hour.

4. In the Work Activity column, list all the activities you performed in an average workweek in the last month, starting underneath "Processing." For some suggestions of common work activities see the list on pages 137–138. (If you have already completed this list in the Advanced Strengths Chart worksheet, you can copy those activities here.)

5. In the Boundary column, define the scope of each work activity. The purpose of doing this is to make sure you've accounted for each activity and there is no overlap in the time you report. For instance, suppose you list both Sales and

Networking separately in the Activity column. In the Boundary column, clarify the difference between the two, such as writing that "making cold calls" applies only to Sales but that time spent in public at various functions is part of the Networking activity.

6. Move to the Current column now. Copy the Current Hours number you came up with before into the small box at the top of the column. You'll need that number for the next step.

7. Now, in the Current column, estimate how many hours in an average workweek you spend in each work activity. Always round to the nearest half-hour.

   a. Notice that Travel has "~50% of total travel" written in the box. This is because usually half of your travel time can be engaged in other activities. Estimate how much time you spend traveling to, from, and during work, divide in half, and then put that number here.

   b. The Processing box is grayed out. Just skip it for now, because—unless you currently have a set time and place for processing every week—you are likely losing more than 25 percent of your day to "processing on the go." You'll have a chance to remedy that pattern through this worksheet!

c.   *Important:* Do *not* try to reconcile the total to your current work hours as you go. Just make your best guess. In the next steps you'll have a chance to clean things up.

8. Add up all your estimates in the Current column, and then subtract the total from your Current hours number at the top. You will likely end up with a number such as +4 or −7.5. (If your estimates exactly add up to your current work hours, then you can skip to step 10.)

9. Now, since there is only one time line and only one you (see *The Myth of Multitasking: How "Doing It All" Gets Nothing Done* for more information on this), you need to bring your time estimates back into balance. Clean up your estimates by adding or subtracting time from different activities or your current work hours estimate until the sum of your estimated activity hours and your estimated total work hours equal each other. These are the typical

culprits for making errors in your work time estimates:

- Over- or underestimating the total number of hours you actually work per week, including not accounting for time working from home.
- Not clearly defining activities in the Boundary column, causing overlap between two or more activities.
- Over- or underestimating the largest blocks of time when you do a particular activity.
- Forgetting an activity and failing to account for it.
- Not accounting for attempting to multitask in your estimates.

10. Take a step back to the $/Hour column. Here, estimate the replacement wage per hour for each activity. The replacement wage per hour is the actual wage per hour you would need to pay someone else to perform this same activity at the same level of effectiveness at which you currently perform it.

11. Take the value of the highest wage per hour and place it in the Processing box. This is because Processing, when done properly, leverages your

ability to stay focused in your Most Valuable Activities.

12. Now return to the first column, the Rank column. Rank each activity according to the replacement wage per hour. Processing is #1 and should be tied with the highest-value activity on your list. The next-highest-value activity should be #2, and so on. Travel and Wasting Time will tie for the lowest-valued activities, since they are worth absolutely nothing!

13. Take a moment to compare the Rank, the $/ Hour, and the Current columns. Does anything stand out to you? Are there very low-value activities that you are spending a lot of time in? Make some conclusions about what you would like to change.

14. Now move to the Vision column. At the very top, just take today's date, add two years, and put that date in the grey box at the top. The next step is to make your work time budget as you would ideally like it to be two years from now.

15. In the small box next to Vision, put the number of hours per week you would like to be work-ing two years from now. Be sure to include travel time to and from work. Do you want to

be working less? More? If there is no change, then just write the same number you have in the Current column.

16. Next, create a new time budget according to how you want your workweek to look two years from now. Reduce the number of hours you will spend in your lowest-value activities and increase the number of hours you will spend in your MVAs—which likely are the highest-ranked activities.

    Important: For the Processing row, the amount of time the average person needs is five hours. You may adjust that as you develop more experience, but start with five hours for now.

17. Make sure that this new Vision work time budget balances out with the hours you intend to be working.

18. Now repeat steps 14 through 17 for the Target column, with one important change. The target is a realistic result that you are going to obtain *one month* from now. So, put a date one month from now in the grey box at the top, and then create a new budget for how you will use your time. An easy way to do this is to look at your Vision column, and see where you would like

Appendix

CURRENT HOURS		STATED VALUE/HOUR		ACTUAL VALUE/HOUR
RANK	ACTIVITY		BOUNDARY	
	Travel		"Engaged" travel to, from, and during work (usually by car)	
	Wasting Time		Non-recreation such as addictions, mindless Web surfing, and so on	
I	Processing		Taking items from gathering points and deciding What, When, and Where	

Sal/Hr							
$/HOUR	CURRENT	HR	VISION	HR	TARGET	HR	☑
$0	~ 50% of total travel						
$0							
~ Value of highest	~ 28% of total						

to be. Then make small increases or decreases in time spent in each activity to nudge you one step closer to that long-term Vision. Again, unless you are sure you need more or less time, put five hours for Processing.

Important: For the Target column, try to make small steps that you absolutely know you can take in the next month toward your long-term Vision. Don't overreach. Remember that many small victories will eventually lead to a large one.

19. Now you're just two steps away from the end! Compare the changes between the Current column and the Target column. For any row that has a change in amount of time spent, tick the column with the checkmark at the top. This note is telling you that you need to take some action to improve your schedule.

20. Finally, for each tick you made, apply the What, When, Where processing system. This causes you to take steps toward improving the amount of time in your MVAs, thereby increasing your value per hour!

SIMPLE WHAT, WHEN, WHERE PROCESSING

Result

This worksheet gives you the basic outline for your regular weekly processing. It will help you take every item in your life and process it properly in an orderly fashion, rather than making decisions "on the fly" and constantly interrupting your day.

Important: This is only a very basic outline of What, When, Where processing, designed to help you begin your own. For a deeper understanding of processing and organization, visit www.DaveCrenshaw. com to learn about Invaluable Personal Coaching.

Steps

1. Locate the worksheet on page 155 and make a copy. Put that copy in a place where you can see it every day while working. You will refer back to this system every time you process, so you want it readily available as a quick resource.
2. Begin practicing using the What, When, Where system by picking up one item that's in your

workspace. *Important:* When processing, only pick up or view *one* item at a time!

3. Answer the first question: *What is the next step?* The "next step" means the next action *you* need to take in order to move this item toward completion. Avoid thinking about any steps beyond just the next one in front of you, which will only confuse you and cause you to try to multitask. Once you have the answer clearly in your head, you're ready to move on.

4. Answer the second question: *When will it be done?* The "it" in this case is not the whole item—just the next step that you decided on. This means you need to make a decision about your schedule. When will you be able to complete the next step? If that next step:

   • Can be completed in less than five minutes, then do it now.

      Why? Because it will take you about that long to document when you will do the step on a calendar or task list, along with the mental cost in time and energy to switch from that task to the next.

   • Will take more than fifteen minutes to complete *or* has a deadline, then schedule it on your calendar.

Why? Because the calendar is a rigid time budget—a commitment you make of where you will spend your time. If you place a long step on a task list, you will continually procrastinate about doing it because you did not budget enough time to complete the step.

- Can be completed in five to fifteen minutes and does not have a deadline, then put it on a task list that can remind you when you intend to do it. Set the reminder time for the date when you think you'll be able to complete that task. (Examples of task lists with reminders include Smartphones, Outlook, and other digital planners.)

  Why? Because the task list is flexible in nature, but you still need something else to do that remembering of when you intend to do that task. Otherwise, you'll forget when you meant to do that task, meaning you'll just have to reprocess this item all over again in the future!

5. Answer the final question: *Where is its home?* A home is any resting place for your items, permanent or temporary. Make a conscious decision where you intend to put the item so that you can find it again later easily. This includes throwing things away that you know you won't need again. Make this a rule: "Everything has a home

and no visitors allowed," which means that items of different types shouldn't be jumbled together. No more "miscellaneous" drawers or piles.

Why? Because it is a tremendous waste of time to have to relocate items that you had and lost. Shuffling through drawers and files and even your computer looking for something is most definitely *not* one of your Most Valuable Activities!

6. If, after taking action on the first step, more action steps remain, then reprocess the item by repeating steps 2 through 5. Repeat until the item is completely resolved.

7. Now that you have processed your first item, build mental muscle memory by practicing again with ten more items, one item at a time. Doing so right now will help you get into the habit. The more you use this system, the faster and more automatic it will become for you.

8. During processing time scheduled in your calendar, use this system for each item that is unprocessed, one item at a time.

What, When, Where Processing

GATHERING POINTS

ONE ITEM AT A TIME

What
is the next step?

When
will it be done?

Where
is its home?

❏ Figure out just NEXT action step, nothing more.

❏ Should this action be OFFLOADED?

❏ Do it now if it can be done in 5 minutes or less.

❏ CALENDAR IT if it:
Will take *more* than 15 minutes
-or-
Has a deadline.

❏ TASK IT if it:
Will take *between* 5 to 15 minutes
-and-
Does *not* have a deadline.

❏ EVERYTHING has a home, and no visitors allowed.

❏ DELETE if you'll never need to see it again.

❏ RESOURCE items using files, boxes, shelves, and digital storage.

REPEAT IF INCOMPLETE

SINGLE PAGE SYSTEM TEMPLATE

Result

This worksheet gives you a template for creating simple systems for your position. By documenting the processes of your position, you become the expert and authority on how the system operates, making you more valuable.

Note: The steps described here assume that *you* are the system expert—the person who best knows how to perform the activity. If you are not the system expert, then you will need to interview the expert to learn how to fill in the different elements of this template.

Steps

1. Locate the template on page 161. Although you can make a copy to practice writing a system, you will want to make your own template using a simple editor such as Microsoft Word or Google Docs.

Bonus: As a thank-you for buying this book, you may download a basic template usable in most document editors for free at www.SinglePageSystem.com.

2. With the Single Page Template you now have, begin in the What section. The What section describes the end result of the system. This should be a brief phrase, one or two sentences at most. This simply describes what the system will accomplish. The sentence may begin either with "This system will . . . " or "To. . . . "

Example: "This system helps greet every visitor to Invaluable, Inc., in a way that makes them feel a part of the family."

3. Continue to the Why section. This is the logic or motivation behind the system. Every business system that you create must have a clear, logical reason for its existence. It is especially helpful to start the Why section in a way that answers the question, "What's in it for an employee to follow this system? What do *they* get from it?"

Example: "By following this system, you'll help your own workday be more enjoyable. Happy customers also buy more, so you'll increase the profitability of the company—which increases your personal profitability."

4. In the Who section, list the positions responsible for following this system. Also, list the managing position responsible for the positions using this system. Be sure to list position titles, *not* names (which may change over time).

   Example: "Office Manager. Results are reported to: VP Operations."

5. Under When, list the standards of this system related to timing and length, such as how often the system should be used, how long it should take to complete the system, how soon follow-up should take place, what time of day is best to use the system, and so on.

   Example: "Customers should be greeted within ten seconds of opening the door." "Follow-up calls should be made within twenty-four hours of order." "Employee-manager huddle meetings should be held twice per month for fifty minutes per meeting."

6. List any numerical or quantifiable standards in the How Much section. If this is a sales system, you'll want to include conversion ratio standards. If this is a product-related system, you'll want to

establish the standard for errors and number of units produced within a given period.

Example: "One out of four people who submit their contact information should eventually make a purchase." "Return rates should not exceed 2 percent." "Customer satisfaction should be assessed on a scale of 1 to 10, with the average being no less than 9.2."

7. For With What, list any resources an employee needs to complete the system.

Example: "QuickBooks; requisition form; pencil; access to the Internet; company credit card; hammer."

8. Last, in the How section, list the action steps in a bullet point or numerical format. *Do not* try to document every last detail of the system. Only create a basic outline of the system for quick reference in the future and an outline for training. By keeping the system outline short and simple, you improve the usage of the system for others.

INVALUABLE ◯ INC.
Systems. Accountability. Motivation.®

SINGLE PAGE
SYSTEM TEMPLATE

| What |
| (Vision or End Result) |

•

| How |
| (System Steps) |

| Why |
| (Motivation or Logic) |

•

| Who |
| (Accountable Positions) |

•

• Results are reported to:

| When |
| (Timing & Length) |

•

| How Much |
| (Measuring Standards) |

•

| With What |
| (Required Resources) |

•

Business
Systems

SYSTEMS MANAGEMENT

FREE INVALUABLE SCORE

Receive a free online assessment to find out how Invaluable you are! Your purchase of this book entitles you to receive one free online Invaluable Score—Light Edition. The Light Edition is a free, basic quick analysis based on the full test we provide to corporate clients at Invaluable, Inc.

This online assessment is an analysis of your current value to your business and market in general. We ask you a series of questions about your work habits, the activities you perform, and your current attitude toward the job you currently have. The Invaluable Score then provides you with a number to measure your progress toward becoming Invaluable.

You'll also receive a set of clear action steps you can take to begin increasing your value per hour and improve focus on your MVAs.

To receive your free assessment, please visit www.InvaluableScore.com.

ACKNOWLEDGMENTS

The development of this book depended upon many individuals:

To all my clients, past and present, business owner and employee alike, who have permitted me to serve you and learn in the process. *Invaluable* combines the stories of so many that it is no longer possible to identify where one story ends and another begins. This is the story of all of you.

To the following sage individuals, who helped build the character and wisdom of Charlie through my experiences and interviews with them:

H. Ray Gibbons
Robert B. Nixon
Arlo Walker

G. Barton Payne
Larry H. Miller
Thelma Crenshaw
Calvin P. Midgley

To Matt Wagner, for his fresh vision and relentless loyalty.

To everyone at Jossey-Bass, for believing in me the first time, and then believing in me again.

To my wife and kids, for everything else.

ABOUT THE AUTHOR

As a highly sought-after speaker, business coach, and productivity expert, Dave Crenshaw has helped thousands of CEOs and employees worldwide gain thousands of hours of productivity yearly and radically increase their value in an ever-evolving market.

Dave received his B.S. in business management-entrepreneurship from Brigham Young University, one of the nation's top entrepreneur programs, and began his coaching career in 1998. His first book, *The Myth of Multitasking: How "Doing It All" Gets Nothing Done,* is a time management best seller available in multiple languages worldwide. He is the founder of

Invaluable, Inc., a coaching and training corporation dedicated to helping companies, their leaders, and their employees become truly invaluable.

Dave lives in the shadow of Utah's Rocky Mountains with his wife and two children.

For more information on Dave Crenshaw and Invaluable, Inc., visit www.InvaluableInc.com.